WHAT SMALL GROUP LEADERS AND MEMBERS ARE SAYING ABOUT EXPERIENCING CHRIST TOGETHER

My group was formed four years ago of very new believers. EXPERIENCING CHRIST TOGETHER has helped form bonds, and we have fallen in love with Christ. We have had many trials, but we have learned to lean on the body of Christ to carry us through the difficult times. I know our lives are richer than ever.

—Leader

The EXPERIENCING CHRIST TOGETHER series has motivated me more than any other Bible study that I have ever been to. This Bible study gets to the heart of the matter—my character in Christ—and that has created action on my part.

—Leader

I love the fact that Jesus' life shows us how to live.

—Member

This series is an "awakening." Jesus has become a very personal friend.

—Leader

This series is definitely a must-do as the foundation for a healthy, maturing small group!

—Leader

EXPERIENCING CHRIST TOGETHER is a safe place to learn about the living Jesus and how he wants to lead us and love us.

—Member

EXPERIENCING CHRIST TOGETHER ties the heart and the mind together. The Bible knowledge grows the mind and the life application grows the heart and transforms the soul.

—Member

Other Studies in the EXPERIENCING CHRIST TOGETHER Series

Beginning in Christ Together (Life of Jesus)

Connecting in Christ Together (Fellowship)

Growing in Christ Together (Discipleship)

Serving Like Christ Together (Ministry)

Sharing Christ Together (Evangelism)

Studies in the DOING LIFE TOGETHER Series

Beginning Life Together (God's Purpose for Your Life)

Connecting with God's Family (Fellowship)

Growing to Be Like Christ (Discipleship)

Developing Your SHAPE to Serve Others (Ministry)

Sharing Your Life Mission Every Day (Evangelism)

Surrendering Your Life to God's Pleasure (Worship)

experiencing
CHRIST
together

SURRENDERING TO CHRIST TOGETHER

six sessions on
Worship

written by
BRETT and DEE EASTMAN
TODD and DENISE WENDORFF
KAREN LEE-THORP

ZONDERVAN™

GRAND RAPIDS, MICHIGAN 49530 USA

We want to hear from you. Please send your comments about this book to us in care of zreview@zondervan.com. Thank you.

ZONDERVAN™

Surrendering to Christ Together
Copyright © 2005 by Brett and Deanna Eastman, Todd and Denise Wendorff, and Karen Lee-Thorp

Requests for information should be addressed to:
Zondervan, *Grand Rapids, Michigan 49530*

ISBN 0-310-24982-1

Interior icons by Tom Clark

Interior design by Beth Shagene & Michelle Espinoza

Printed in the United States of America

05 06 07 08 09 10 11 /❖ DCI/ 10 9 8 7 6 5 4 3 2 1

CONTENTS

EXPERIENCING CHRIST TOGETHER

EXPERIENCING CHRIST TOGETHER: LIVING WITH PURPOSE IN COMMUNITY will take you face to face with Jesus himself. In addition to being the Son of God and Savior of the world, Jesus holds the greatest wisdom and understands the purposes for which God formed you. He knows what it takes to build authentic relationships, to know God more intensely, to grow spiritually, and ultimately to make a difference in the world. EXPERIENCING CHRIST TOGETHER offers you a chance to do what Jesus' first followers did: spend time with him, listen to what he said, watch what he did, and pattern your life after his.

Jesus lived every moment following God's purpose for his life. In this study you will experience firsthand how he did this and how you can do it too. Yet if you're anything like us, knowing what God wants for you is one thing, but doing it is something else. That's why you'll follow Jesus' plan of doing life not alone but together. As you follow in his footsteps, you'll find his pathway more exciting than anything you've imagined.

Book 1 of this series (*Beginning in Christ Together*) explores the person of Jesus Christ. Each of the subsequent five studies looks through Jesus' eyes at one of God's five biblical purposes for his people (fellowship, discipleship, service, evangelism, and worship). For example, *Surrendering to Christ Together* is about worship. Book 1 is about grace: what Christ has done for us. The other books are about how we live in response to grace.

Even if you've done another LIFE TOGETHER study, you'll be amazed at how Jesus can take you to places of faith you've never been before. The joy of life in him is far beyond a life you could design on your own. If you do all six study guides in this series, you'll spend one astonishing year with Jesus Christ.

Extreme Faith

One thing that fascinates us about Jesus and his disciples is their drastic commitment to the Father's agenda, both for them as individuals and the world as a whole. Like athletes in extreme sports, they don't let little things like mortal danger keep them from going for the gold. From our safe seats as spectators, we watch them snowboard down spiritual mountains and wonder where they get the guts to give it their all.

We call such total abandonment to the Father's plan "surrender." In *Surrendering to Christ Together*, you'll explore six heart attitudes that can motivate you to surrender to God's agenda: faith in God's power and wisdom; passion to have your life count for something; humility; wild gratitude; commitment stronger than the costs; and confidence in your eternal survival. Because worship is the only sensible response to what you'll learn about God, we've also packed this study with creative ideas that we hope will take your group to new depths of worship.

If you've been holding back something from God for fear of failure or loss, or because you're too busy pursuing your own goals, take a good look at what motivated Jesus and his closest friends. You might find out that extreme faith is for you too.

Outline of Each Session

Most people want to live healthy, balanced spiritual lives, but few achieve this alone. And most small groups struggle to balance all of God's purposes in their meetings. Groups tend to overemphasize one of the five purposes, perhaps fellowship or discipleship. Rarely is there a healthy balance that includes evangelism, ministry, and worship. That's why we've included all of these elements in this study so you can live a healthy, balanced spiritual life over time.

A typical group session will include the following:

 CONNECTING WITH GOD'S FAMILY (FELLOWSHIP). The foundation for spiritual growth is an intimate connection with God and his family. A few people who really know you and who earn your trust provide a place to experience the life Jesus invites you to live. This section of each session typically offers you two options. You can get to know your whole group by using the icebreaker question (always question 1), or you can check in with one or two group members— your spiritual partner(s)—for a deeper connection and encouragement in your spiritual journey.

DVD TEACHING SEGMENT. A DVD companion to this study guide is available. For each study session, a teacher discusses the topic, ordinary Christians talk about the personal experience of the topic, a scholar gives background on the Bible passage, and a leadership coach gives tips to the group leader. The DVD contains worship helps and other features as well. If you are using the DVD, you will view the teaching segment after your Connecting discussion and before your Bible study (the Growing section). At the end of each session in this study guide you will find space for your notes on the teaching segment. To view a sample of the DVD, log on to www.lifetogether.com/ ExperiencingChristTogether.

GROWING TO BE LIKE CHRIST (DISCIPLESHIP). Here is where you come face to face with Christ. In a core Bible passage you'll see Jesus in action, teaching or demonstrating some aspect of how he wants you to live. The focus won't be on accumulating information but on how Jesus' words and actions relate to what you say and do. We want to help you apply the Scriptures practically, creatively, and from your heart as well as your head. At the end of the day, allowing the timeless truths from God's Word to transform our lives in Christ is our greatest aim.

FOR DEEPER STUDY. If you want to dig deeper into more Bible passages about the topic at hand, we've provided additional passages and questions. Your group may choose to do study homework ahead of each meeting in order to cover more biblical material. Or you as an individual may choose to study the For Deeper Study passages on your own. If you prefer not to do study homework, the Growing section will provide you with plenty to discuss within the group. These options allow individuals or the whole group to go deeper in their study, while still accommodating those who can't do homework or are new to your group.

You can record your discoveries on the Reflections page at the end of each session. We encourage you to read some of your insights to a friend (spiritual partner) for accountability and support. Spiritual partners may check in each week over the phone, through email, or at the beginning of the group meeting.

DEVELOPING YOUR GIFTS TO SERVE OTHERS (MINISTRY). Jesus trained his disciples to discover and develop their gifts to serve others. God has designed you uniquely to serve him in a way no other person can. This section will help you discover and use your God-given design. It will also encourage your group to discover your unique design as a community. In two sessions in this study, you'll put into practice what you've learned in the Bible study by taking a step to serve others. These simple steps will take your group on a faith journey that could change your lives forever.

 SHARING YOUR LIFE MISSION EVERY DAY (EVANGELISM). Many people skip over this aspect of the Christian life because it's scary, relationally awkward, or simply too much work for their busy schedules. But Jesus wanted all of his disciples to help outsiders connect with him, to know him personally. This doesn't mean preaching on street corners. It could mean welcoming a few newcomers into your group, hosting a short-term group in your home, participating in a cross-cultural missions project, or walking through this study with a friend. In four sessions of this study, you'll have an opportunity to take a small step in this area. These steps will take you beyond Bible study to Bible living.

 SURRENDERING YOUR LIFE FOR GOD'S PLEASURE (WORSHIP). God is most pleased by a heart that is fully his. Each group session will give you a chance to surrender your heart to God in prayer and worship. You may read a psalm together, share a page in your journal, or use one of the songs on the DVD to open or close your meeting. (Additional music is available on the LIFE TOGETHER Worship DVD/CD series, produced by Maranatha!) If you've never prayed aloud in a group before, no one will put pressure on you. Instead, you'll experience the support of others who are praying for you. This time will knit your hearts in community and help you surrender all your hurts and dreams into the hands of the One who knows you best.

STUDY NOTES. This section provides background notes on the Bible passage(s) you examine in the Growing section. You may want to refer to these notes during your group meeting or as a reference for those doing additional study.

REFLECTIONS. At the end of each session is a blank page on which you can write your insights from your personal time with God. Whether you do deeper Bible study, read through the gospel of John or the Psalms, meditate on a few verses, or simply write out your prayers, you'll benefit from writing down what you discover. You may want to pick up a blank journal or notepad after you fill in these pages.

AFLOAT IN A STORM

Andrea's husband came home with the news that he had lost his job. They had their lives planned for many years: they loved the area, their kids' school, the kids' youth programs, their ministry in the church, and their friendships at church. They'd had no intention of moving, but he would be out of work in three months. Three months! How could anyone find a new job so fast in a down economy?

Days later, Andrea's small group called a prayer time for her family. She was embarrassed and canceled it. She didn't want to be the sole recipient of all their prayers; she was embarrassed to take time out of everyone's day just to pray for her. But the group pushed and pushed until she committed to a date and time.

When the group met, one member had put together a page-long list of items to pray for, including everything from a new job to peace, from increased awareness of God's care to finances. The list was humbling to read. They had thought of everything Andrea could possibly worry about or question as she faced the next few months. Andrea sensed God's gentle voice showing her that these people were his physical arms around her as her family faced their loss and looked ahead for new direction. Through these people, God would keep her afloat as she weathered the storm.

CONNECTING WITH GOD'S FAMILY   20 min.

A life oriented toward worshiping God, surrendering to him, begins with trust. To what degree do we trust God to care for us and those we love, regardless of circumstances? Different personalities have different natural responses to tough circumstances, both in the short run and over the long haul. It's helpful to know what comes naturally to different members of your group.

   1. How do you typically respond when trouble hits your life? (Select all that apply.)

- ☐ I panic.
- ☐ I worry.
- ☐ I become unemotional and focus on handling things.
- ☐ I handle a short crisis well, but if the painful situation goes on and on, it's hard for me to persevere.
- ☐ I freeze up in a sudden crisis, but if the painful situation goes on, I pull myself together for a potential marathon.
- ☐ I become hyperactive.
- ☐ I distract myself with food, entertainment, the Internet, work, shopping, or _____.
- ☐ I talk to friends.
- ☐ I isolate myself.
- ☐ I get depressed.
- ☐ I pray.
- ☐ I ask people for help.
- ☐ Other: _____

2. Whether your group is brand new or ongoing, it's always important to reflect on and review your values together. On pages 72–73 is a sample agreement with the values we've found most useful in sustaining healthy, balanced groups. We recommend that you choose one or two values—ones you haven't previously focused on or have room to grow in—to emphasize during this study. Choose ones that will take your group to the next stage of intimacy and spiritual health.

   ☐ *For new groups:* A study on surrender may prompt group members to share areas of their lives they want to surrender more deeply to God. This is private information that requires a high level of trust, so two values you might want to emphasize are "safe environment" and "confidentiality."

   ☐ *For existing groups:* If you feel that the trust level in your group is already high, you can go the next step by emphasizing "spiritual partners." Partners can check in with each other weekly to encourage one another in surrendering to God more deeply and maintaining a vibrant personal time with him. If the idea of spiritual partners is new to you, you'll learn more about it in session 2.

GROWING TO BE LIKE CHRIST   40 min.

Several of Jesus' disciples were professional fishermen. They had spent years on the Sea of Galilee and had been through countless storms. But one evening, crossing the sea with Jesus, the disciples found themselves in a squall that made them panic.

Storms happen. Becoming followers of Jesus doesn't change that fact, but it does offer new ways to think about and respond to storms—if we're willing.

3. Read Mark 4:35–41. Describe the scene:

Who was there?

What did the disciples do when the waves started breaking over the boat?

Why did they respond that way?

4. Why do you think they questioned Christ's care for them (verse 38)?

5. Jesus said his followers' fear reflected a lack of faith (verse 40). Faith means belief or trust. What should they have believed or trusted?

6. What would a faith-filled response to the storm have been?

7. What did the disciples learn about Jesus from this experience?

8. How is this story relevant to the storms—large and small—that we encounter in life?

9. If we know Jesus has authority even over the wind and waves, why is it still hard for many of us to trust him when painful or discouraging events occur?

10. What current situation is challenging you to trust Jesus and/or persevere through pain?

FOR DEEPER STUDY

Read Mark 8:1–21. What do the disciples have trouble trusting about Jesus in this passage? What reasons for their lack of trust does Jesus give?

What does Paul urge the Colossians to believe about Jesus in Colossians 1:15–22? Why are these things so important to trust— not just intellectually, but at our core—when we go through life's storms? What in this passage motivates you to surrender your worries to Christ?

SURRENDERING YOUR LIFE FOR GOD'S PLEASURE 15–30 min.

11. Pray for those who mentioned difficult situations in question 10. You might want to gather around a person and place your hands on his or her shoulders to communicate your support while you pray.

12. The Prayer and Praise Report on page 19 is a good place to keep track of the group's prayer requests and answers to prayer. Are there any additional requests you'd like the group to pray for this week?

13. A regular habit of worship can build our trust in God because it focuses our attention on what makes him trustworthy. Worship strengthens us for the long haul. Here are two ideas for responding to this study with worship:

☐ Read Psalm 31 aloud together. If you want to be creative, let half your group say the odd-numbered verses and the other half say the even-numbered ones. (In a couple's group, let the men and women be the two sets of speakers.) When you finish, allow some open time for group members to add their own words of praise, perhaps based on things that struck them from the psalm.

☐ Use a song from the DVD, the LIFE TOGETHER Worship series, or a CD of your choice, to worship God with music. Play a song once while the group simply listens prayerfully, perhaps with eyes closed. Play it again with the volume loud enough that people will feel comfortable singing.

14. Following are several options for cultivating a surrendered heart on a daily basis. Select one or two that fit where you are in your spiritual growth process.

☐ **Prayer.** Commit to praying daily during this study about an area of your life that you want to surrender more deeply to God. Each morning or evening, surrender that issue. Ask God to empower you to persevere in whatever action he wants you to take. You may find it helpful to write your prayer in a notebook or on the Reflections page (page 30).

☐ **Worship.** Set a goal to increase your practice of worship during the six weeks of this study. Attend a worship service weekly (you could even invite other group members to go as a group and sit together). Plan ten minutes a day of private worship. You could play a worship CD in your car and sing along, write down a list of things for which you are thankful to God, or read a psalm aloud. All of the psalms are excellent for worship; a few to start with are Psalms 89, 92, 95–98, 103, 104, 111, 136, 138, and 145–150.

☐ **Bible Reading.** On pages 85–86 are two options for daily Bible reading. We recommend that you jot down your thoughts about these readings on the Reflections page or in a journal.

☐ **Meditation.** Try meditation as a way of internalizing God's Word more deeply. Copy a portion of each week's Bible study passage onto a card, and tape it somewhere in your line of sight, such as on your car's dashboard or the kitchen table. Think about it when you sit at red lights, or while you're eating a meal. What is God saying to you, here and now, through these words? Several alternative passages for meditation are suggested on the Reflections page in each session. You may use that page to write your responses.

On pages 32–33 is a Personal Health Plan, a chart for keeping track of your progress. In the box that says, "WHAT is your next step for growth?" write the option you chose.

15. Many groups find they're having such a good time with each other that they don't want to open their circle to new people. Why "start over" with a stranger when you already have enough friends? But when you were a stranger to God, and he already had all the love he needed, he widened the circle of his love to include you. Opening your group from time to time is a way of surrendering the group to God so he can use it for his purposes.

Who are the people in your life who need a group like yours? The "Circles of Life" diagram at the bottom of this page will help you think of people in various areas of your life. Prayerfully write down at least three or four names in the circles.

Which of these people will you invite to join your group? Don't hesitate—most people are honored to be invited even if they can't join.

CIRCLES OF LIFE

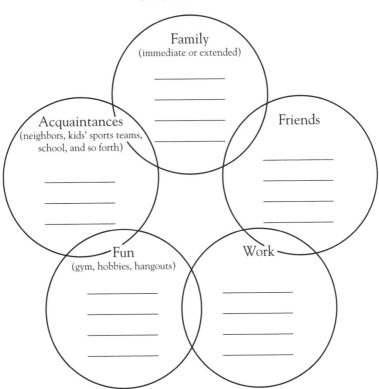

STUDY NOTES

If we drown (Mark 4:38). Because the disciples were seasoned fishermen, they probably weren't overreacting to the storm from a natural point of view. They knew a dangerous storm when they saw it. Yet Jesus had said they were going to the other side of the sea (verse 35). The disciples used a strong word to describe their predicament: *apollumi,* which means to fully be destroyed. Did they really believe this was the end?

No faith (4:40). To Jesus, faith (trust) was everything. This wasn't the only time he pointed out his disciples' lack of faith (see 7:18; 8:17–18, 21, 32–33; 9:19). The word usage in 4:40 indicates that the disciples should have been further along in their faith journeys than their behavior showed. John Bisagno writes, "Faith is not believing God can. Faith is believing God will."[1] When our confidence in the One who can calm the storm is greater than our confidence in ourselves, real surrender happens. In whom do you place your faith?

The wind and the waves obey him (4:41). Jesus is the Creator and Master over all created things, even the wind and sea. (See Psalm 65:5–13; 107:25; Colossians 1:15–17).

---

[1]John Bisagno, *The Power of Positive Praying* (Grand Rapids: Zondervan, 1965), 14

PRAYER AND PRAISE REPORT

Briefly share your prayer requests with the large group, making notations below. Then gather in smaller groups of two to four to pray for each other.

Date: _____

Prayer Requests

_____

_____

_____

_____

_____

_____

_____

_____

_____

_____

Praise Report

_____

_____

_____

_____

_____

_____

_____

_____

_____

_____

REFLECTIONS

Use this page to write out your prayers, your thoughts about your daily Bible reading, or your meditations on a verse from the passage you have already studied. Below are some suggested verses for meditation. The Bible Reading Plans are on pages 85–86.

For Meditation: Mark 4:38–41 or 4:40–41

DVD NOTES

If you are watching the accompanying *Surrendering to Christ Together* DVD, write down what you sense God saying to you through the speaker. (If you'd like to hear a sample of the DVD teaching segment, go to www.lifetogether.com/ExperiencingChristTogether.)

_____

_____

_____

_____

_____

_____

_____

_____

_____

_____

_____

_____

_____

_____

_____

_____

_____

_____

_____

_____

_____

_____

_____

_____

_____

THE KEY TO SIGNIFICANCE

Melanie was pursuing her Ph.D. when she found out she was pregnant. Academic achievement had been her first priority. She had always said, "I'll never have kids. I was not meant to be a mom!"

But soon she found herself diapering a wailing baby who swathed her in sour-milk spit-up. Far from the world of graduate studies, Melanie loathed her new role. Her mother suggested, "Why don't you get to know other stay-at-home moms?"

But Melanie refused to become a member of the sorority of "stay-at-home moms." The title made her cringe. A year and a half later she remained friendless. Her despair deepened.

When acquaintances asked her to become part of a playgroup, Melanie's self-reliant heart nearly uttered, "No thanks." But she decided to become part of these mothers' small group. The first night, Sue, a calm, kind woman, shared how she was seeking counseling for anger. *Anger?* Melanie thought. *Other mothers—Christian mothers—are angry too?*

Kristin disclosed her struggle with depression and need for medication. Melanie was thunderstruck.

Moved by the group's honesty and gentleness, Melanie blurted out, "I'm depressed. I can't handle life. I yell at my child. My husband and I are fighting. I cry all the time. My life is purposeless. I need help."

The group prayed for her. A week later she was speaking to the same counselor who was helping Sue. Weekly Melanie returned to her group for prayer as she inched her way through depression.

Melanie's woes gradually lessened. Mothering still wasn't something she relished as much as her previous academic life. But she accepted it and even began to find fulfillment in it.

CONNECTING WITH GOD'S FAMILY   10 min.

1. Instead of having one person offer an opening prayer, begin your meeting with some time for everyone to pray briefly. Each person may pray one or two sentences (please, no sermons).

Don't go in a circle because that might put pressure on those who would rather not pray aloud. Let the leader close when things slow down.

Focus your prayers on things you want to put into the Father's hands. For example:

- ☐ Father, I surrender to you my tough week at work.
- ☐ Lord, thanks for helping us this week with our son.
- ☐ Jesus, we need your help in finding a job.

 ## GROWING TO BE LIKE CHRIST   40 min.

In the first session we saw that faith (trust) is the number-one motivator to help us surrender to God's agenda. The next motive we'll explore is significance. Significance means having our lives count for something. Most of us have goals or dreams of doing something that matters. Dreams are good; having no dreams is called despair.

The catch is this: often our goals conflict with God's agenda. Then we have to decide, will I surrender my goal or set aside God's agenda? Sometimes surrendering our goal feels like the obvious and sensible thing to do. At other times it feels like the death of a dream or a threat to our very survival. Jesus knew exactly how hard it could be, because surrender to his Father had set him on a path toward a horrible death. Why did Jesus go through with it?

2. Read John 12:23–28. What point does Jesus make about his life by comparing it to a kernel of wheat?

3. How should we see our lives as grains of wheat?

4. What does Jesus mean when he says, "The man who loves his life will lose it" (verse 25)? (See the Study Notes on page 28.)

5. In verse 25, "hate" means indifference compared with the things we passionately love. In what ways should a person "hate his life" for Jesus' sake?

6. Suppose someone said, "Maybe wheat has to die to produce more wheat, and maybe Jesus had to die in order to bring something priceless to the world, but why do I have to 'die' in order for my life to be significant?" How would you respond?

7. Jesus felt the emotional turmoil anyone would feel when facing a brutal death (verses 27–28). What helped him stay on course despite his emotions?

8. Read Luke 9:22–27, 57–62. Jesus had known for some time that he was heading for death. He had been warning his followers of the costs and rewards of committing themselves to him. What costs of following him does Jesus promise here?

What rewards does he promise?

9. Have you ever known someone who gained "the whole world"—or at least a lot of what he thought would make him happy—yet lost "his very self" (Luke 9:25)? Why did that happen?

10. Jesus wants even our good earthly goals to be secondary to his agenda. Consider the following goals. Which, if any, do you love too much? How do you do that?

☐ Career advancement
☐ Career achievement
☐ Career enjoyment
☐ Family prosperity
☐ Children who grow up to be happy and successful
☐ Respect or status in your social group

FOR DEEPER STUDY

Does Jesus' teaching about hating our lives in this world mean that most of what we do all day (work at an ordinary job, raise a family, and so on) is almost worthless in God's eyes? Explain your view on this in light of Scripture. How can we "die" and be fruitful like wheat *within* our daily labors?

In Matthew 10:39; 16:25; Mark 8:35; and Luke 17:33, Jesus repeats the same idea of loving/hating, finding/losing one's life in different ways. Read each of these in context. What additional insights do you get from these passages about how to gain real life? Why do you suppose Jesus talked about this theme so often?

The apostle Paul talked about losing and finding his life too. Read Acts 22:1–22 and Philippians 3:4–14. What did Paul lose? What did he gain? Why couldn't he have gained those things and accomplished what he did without losing so much?

SURRENDERING YOUR LIFE FOR GOD'S PLEASURE   15–30 min.

11. Pair up with someone in your group. (We suggest that men partner with men and women with women.) This person will be your "spiritual partner" during this study. If you have a spiritual partner from another study in this series, you can keep the same partner or switch.

   Turn to your Personal Health Plan on pages 32–33. In the box that says, "WHO are you connecting with spiritually?" write your partner's name.

   Tell your partner what step you chose in session 1. On page 33 you also can keep track of your partner's chosen step and record his or her progress when you check with one another each week.

   It's okay to have two partners. If you have two, an additional health plan is on pages 80–81 in the Appendix. Also, on pages 82–83 you'll find a completed health plan filled in as an example.

12. Now look at the Surrender section of your health plan. Find the question, "HOW are you surrendering your heart?" Talk with your partner about this. In what area of your life is God calling you to surrender? It might be something you worry about. It could be something that you put ahead of eternal things. It could even be something positive that God wants you to do with your life. Use the health plan to record your partner's response as well as your own.

13. Pray for your partner.

DEVELOPING YOUR GIFTS FOR SERVICE   10 min.

14. Worship is an essential element of surrender. If you want to strengthen your group's practice of worship over time, the best step you can take is to have one or two members volunteer to champion worship for the group. They don't need to commit to this task forever—they might try out the job for six weeks. Ask for volunteers.

There are many practical ways to champion worship in a group. Here are a few ideas to get you started:

☐ Maintain the group's Prayer and Praise Report. Ask spiritual partners if they have any prayer requests they'd like the whole group to know about. Check in with people to find out whether and how prayers have been answered. When a prayer is answered, update the group.

☐ Select one or more worship songs on the DVD or the LIFE TOGETHER Worship series. Play a song for the group to listen to and worship God silently. When they've learned the words, lead them in singing along.

☐ Select psalms for the group to read aloud.

☐ Plan an outdoor worship experience. (Ideas are on pages 92–93.)

☐ Plan a time to share the Lord's Supper (Communion) together.

☐ Organize the group to attend a weekend worship service together.

☐ Plan a "wild gratitude" worship experience for session 4 (see page 46).

☐ Organize a day of fasting for your group. (You could agree to skip one meal, two meals, or all meals for twenty-four hours. End your fast during your regular group meeting with a simple meal of bread and cheese because meat is hard on the stomach after a fast.)

☐ Throw a birthday party for Jesus (around Christmastime) or a resurrection party (around Easter, or anytime).

STUDY NOTES

Glorified (John 12:23). Jesus spoke these words a few days before his arrest. He referred to his upcoming torture and death as the event in which his divine glory (majesty) would be revealed. By our words and actions, we too can experience God's glory/magnificence and reveal it to others (John 12:28; 17:17–24).

Loves his life . . . hates his life (12:25). Jesus uses "love" and "hate" as relative terms. Compared to our passionate love for eternal life, we should hate the things that sustain only earthly life. Possessions, physical beauty, social status, and even health and physical safety should be lower on our priority list than eternal things like intimacy with God, love for other people, and drawing others toward God. Even Christians often live as though earthly life is all there is and earthly happiness is the highest goal. But Jesus endured death because he knew that to make earthly happiness our highest goal is to miss the point of life. Real, robust life that starts now and stretches into eternity is found only when we are willing to risk losing the things we cling to for earthly happiness.

We are on this earth for such a short time. Yet if we use that time wisely, it's the beginning of eternity. What we accomplish for Christ in this life will last for eternity.

Bury my father (Luke 9:59). The people Jesus rebukes in Luke 9:57–62 are pursuing good goals. This man wants to show respect for his family. Yet Jesus wants even our good goals to be secondary to his agenda.

PRAYER AND PRAISE REPORT

Briefly share your prayer requests with the large group, making notations below. Then gather in smaller groups of two to four to pray for each other.

Date: _____

Prayer Requests

_____

_____

_____

_____

_____

_____

_____

_____

_____

_____

Praise Report

_____

_____

_____

_____

_____

_____

_____

_____

_____

_____

REFLECTIONS

Use this page to write out your prayers, your thoughts about your daily Bible reading, or your meditations on a verse from the passage you have already studied. Below are some suggested verses for meditation. The Bible Reading Plans are on pages 85–86.

For Meditation: John 15:12–13 or 15:9–14

_____

_____

_____

_____

_____

_____

_____

_____

_____

_____

_____

_____

_____

_____

_____

_____

_____

_____

_____

_____

_____

_____

DVD NOTES

If you are watching the accompanying *Surrendering to Christ Together* DVD, write down what you sense God saying to you through the speaker. (If you'd like to hear a sample of the DVD teaching segment, go to www.lifeto-gether.com/ExperiencingChristTogether.)

PERSONAL HEALTH PLAN

This worksheet could become your single most important feature in this study. On it you can record your personal priorities before the Father. It will help you live a healthy spiritual life, balancing all five of God's purposes.

PURPOSE	PLAN
CONNECT	WHO are you connecting with spiritually?
GROW	WHAT is your next step for growth?
DEVELOP	WHERE are you serving?
SHARE	WHEN are you shepherding another in Christ?
SURRENDER	HOW are you surrendering your heart?

If you have more than one partner, another Personal Health Plan can be found in the Appendix or downloaded in a larger format at www.lifeto-gether.com/healthplan. A Sample Health Plan is also in the Appendix.

DATE	MY PROGRESS	PARTNER'S PROGRESS

TRUE GREATNESS

For every person who experiences what the world considers success, many others have sacrificed—usually without publicity—to make that success possible.

Kirk and Molly had two kids and two careers: Kirk was a bond salesman for an investment banking firm and Molly was a nurse. Shortly after their youngest entered first grade, a New York firm recruited Kirk to lead its municipal bonds team. It was the call-up of a lifetime.

But Molly had been dreaming about getting her teaching certificate. She was dead-set against the move. It meant giving up their life in the Chicago suburbs and probably her dream to teach. No matter where they moved in the New York City area, Kirk's commute to the city would be at least two to three hours a day. They prayed about the decision, but there was no consensus.

After a heated discussion, Molly finally agreed to move. But God had been working on Kirk, who began realizing how much Molly had already sacrificed for his career: the nights home with the kids while he worked on his MBA and the long weekends alone while he studied. Kirk decided to turn down the job; it was Molly's turn, he said. God had called him to a different kind of greatness.

CONNECTING WITH GOD'S FAMILY   10 min.

1. Who is one of your heroes? What do you admire about that person?

GROWING TO BE LIKE CHRIST   40 min.

John the Baptist was a hero to many of the people who became Jesus' disciples. He had a thriving ministry with national fame. He was loaded with vision, energy, and entrepreneurial initiative. In fact, he was such a celebrity that the authorities in Jerusalem sent

a delegation to find out who he thought he was. Status was as important in John's time as it is today, so John's attitude toward his hero/celebrity status astounded everyone.

Jesus publicly esteemed John, saying, "Among those born of women there is no one greater than John" (Luke 7:28). But then, to further turn the crowd's expectations upside down, Jesus went on, "yet the one who is least in the kingdom of God is greater than he." Both John and Jesus wanted their disciples to rethink their views of greatness.

2. Read John 1:19–34. How does John describe his mission in life (see verse 23)?

3. What signs of humility do you see in John?

4. Read John 3:22–30. How do John's disciples react when they see Jesus building his ministry?

5. How is John's response different?

6. Often, the more gifted we are with vision and potential for achievement, the more tempted we are to seek status through our achievements. Why do you suppose status-seeking is so tempting?

7. John's attitude was "He [Jesus] must become greater; I must become less" (3:30). Where can you apply this attitude in your life?

FOR DEEPER STUDY

Investigate John's birth and ministry in Luke 1:5–25, 57–80; 3:1–20. What signs of John's greatness do you see? Also, what would you say was important to John, and what wasn't important?

Read Jesus' opinion of John in Luke 7:28. What do you think Jesus means? By what standard does Jesus measure greatness?

Luke 14:11 is a saying Jesus repeated often. It's a core principle of God's kingdom. Why do you think God's kingdom operates like this?

What similar ideas do Paul and James express in Romans 12:3 and James 4:6, respectively?

DEVELOPING YOUR GIFTS FOR SERVICE   20 min.

People oriented toward surrendering to God aren't passive. Their humility doesn't mean they think they have no abilities to offer in service. Rather, like John, they look for what God wants done in the world and listen for his marching orders. John knew his job was to prepare people for Christ, and he pursued that ministry energetically. Surrender for John wasn't just giving up his own agenda; it was being faithful to God's agenda.

There are no five easy steps to discerning God's mission for your life. Discernment comes when you invest time in relationship with God and his family. It comes when you stop to consider: What is God doing? Where is the wind of the Holy Spirit blowing? How can I join him in his work?

8. Gather with your spiritual partner(s). If your partner is absent, you may join another individual or pair. Ask God to guide your conversation on the following questions:

   • Where is God at work around you? How does he want you to be involved?
   • What gifts for service do you see in your partner? What are his or her strengths?
   • Are you tempted to seek status through ministry or other achievements? If so, what steps can you take to serve out of faithfulness rather than for status? How can you let God increase while you decrease?

SURRENDERING YOUR LIFE FOR GOD'S PLEASURE   15–30 min.

9. How can the group pray for you this week?

10. In session 2 you asked for volunteers to plan worship for your group. Allow some time for worship, led by those people.

STUDY NOTES

John (John 1:19). John was the greatest prophet the Jews had seen in centuries. The Jews gave converts a ritual bath to symbolize cleansing from pagan sin. John created a stir when he started giving the ritual bath (baptism) to Jews as a sign that they too needed to be cleansed from sin.

I am not the Christ (1:20). Many Jews were eagerly awaiting the Christ, the Savior-King who they thought would overthrow the Romans and restore Israel as God's kingdom. The authorities in Jerusalem were quick to investigate anyone who might claim to be the Christ. Some of John's fans wanted him to claim the title; John resisted that temptation.

Elijah . . . Prophet (1:21). These were two other figures for whom many Jews of Jesus' day were looking. Moses had promised, "The LORD your God will raise up for you a prophet like me [Moses] from among your own brothers" (Deuteronomy 18:15). Some Jews of Jesus' day thought this Prophet would be the Christ, while others distinguished between the Prophet and the Christ. Likewise, the prophet Malachi had predicted that the prophet Elijah (from the ninth century BC) would return before the "day of the LORD" (Malachi 4:5), which was commonly understood as the day when the Christ would bring judgment to the world. Elijah would be the Christ's forerunner. John denied being either of these great figures, but Jesus said that while John wasn't literally the reincarnation of Elijah, he fulfilled the Elijah role (Matthew 11:13–14). John refused all titles that would have led the people to focus on him instead of Jesus.

The Lamb of God (1:29). John recognized that Jesus was the suffering servant prophesied in Isaiah 53:7. He would become the ultimate Passover lamb (Exodus 12:1–28), whose blood would deliver his people from eternal slavery and death (1 Peter 1:19).

PRAYER AND PRAISE REPORT

Briefly share your prayer requests with the large group, making notations below. Then gather in smaller groups of two to four to pray for each other.

Date: _____

Prayer Requests

_____

_____

_____

_____

_____

_____

_____

_____

_____

_____

Praise Report

_____

_____

_____

_____

_____

_____

_____

_____

_____

_____

REFLECTIONS

Use this page to write out your prayers, your thoughts about your daily Bible reading, or your meditations on a verse from the passage you have already studied. Below are some suggested verses for meditation. The Bible Reading Plans are on pages 85–86.

For Meditation: John 1:26–27, 3:27–30, or 3:30

DVD NOTES

If you are watching the accompanying *Surrendering to Christ Together* DVD, write down what you sense God saying to you through the speaker. (If you'd like to hear a sample of the DVD teaching segment, go to www.lifetogether.com/ExperiencingChristTogether.)

_____

_____

_____

_____

_____

_____

_____

_____

_____

_____

_____

_____

_____

_____

_____

_____

_____

_____

_____

_____

_____

_____

_____

_____

_____

_____

_____

WILD GRATITUDE

Ron Thompson is a rich man. For years Thompson Builders put up forty upscale homes a year and saw millions of dollars of annual profits. "Retirement is for losers," said Ron, and he kept driving hard.

One summer, he was asked to join a mission trip to India to help build a missions compound. Ron had always avoided missions trips—they simply didn't interest him. But the India experience overwhelmed him. Instead of building million-dollar homes for lawyers and doctors, he was building a gated compound for eight hundred orphans, all of whom sat in silence the day he entered their humble quarters for the first time.

No one would describe Ron as rash, but the experience prompted him to turn over his business to one of his sons more quickly than he had planned. Since then, Ron has poured his life into providing housing for those without it in both North America and abroad. He travels a great deal each year, and even as his health deteriorates—he had a triple bypass recently—he keeps on. Not long ago he provided the money for an overseas orphan to have surgery on a club foot, thus enabling the child to walk.

"I've spent my life making a lot of money," he says. "My family and I have so much. I'm now seventy, and I'm going to spend whatever time God has left for me serving those in need."

CONNECTING WITH GOD'S FAMILY   10 min.

A great way to open this study would be to have everyone relax, close their eyes, and listen to one of the songs on the DVD or the LIFE TOGETHER Worship series. You may sing the second time through as a group, or just take a few moments of silence to focus on God and transition out of the distractions of your day.

After that, you may check in as a whole group (question 1) or let spiritual partners check in one-on-one (question 2).

1. What is one thing God has done for which you are wildly grateful?

Or,

2. Sit with your spiritual partner(s). If your partner is absent, you may join another individual or pair. What has the Lord been showing you in your personal time with him? You might share something from your journal.

GROWING TO BE LIKE CHRIST   40 min.

We've talked about surrender based on trust, on a desire to do something with your life that really matters, and on the fact that Christ deserves to be number one. A fourth heart attitude that motivates surrender over the long haul is gratitude. Why does Christ deserve to be at the center of everything we do? Because when we grasp who he is and what he does for us, we aren't just grateful in words. We respond with full surrender of our lives.

Mary of Bethany understood this. Jesus let her sit at his feet as a disciple—an honor rabbis reserved for men only (Luke 10:38–42). Even more remarkable, Jesus raised Mary's brother Lazarus from the dead (John 11:1–44). Mary knew that rescuing her brother from death put Jesus in such danger from the authorities that he had to stay in hiding to avoid arrest (John 11:45–57). Then, a few days before Passover, Jesus arrived back in Bethany. From there he was heading to Jerusalem, where Mary knew he would almost certainly be arrested and killed.

In Bethany, Mary's family attended a dinner with Jesus. She knew this might be the last time she saw him. Without words, her farewell demonstrated her heart of gratitude.

3. Read Mark 14:1–11 and John 12:1–11. These are two accounts of the same event. Describe the context in which this dinner took place. What was going on before, after, and around the dinner?

4. What impression do you get from Mark about why some of the guests were shocked at Mary's action during the dinner (Mark 14:3–5)?

5. According to John, what was Judas's reason for protesting (John 12:4–6)?

6. Why did Jesus think Mary's action was good and appropriate (Mark 14:6–9; John 12:7–8)?

7. What do you think Mary was trying to express through her action?

8. Why do you suppose neither embarrassment nor expense stopped her from this display?

9. How would you compare your own thoughts and emotions about Jesus to Mary's?

10. Jesus died on the cross for our sins. Why do you suppose many Christians don't walk around wildly grateful to him for doing that?

11. In addition to the cross, what has Jesus done that deserves extravagant love, gratitude, or worship from you?

12. It's not difficult to go wild with gratitude for a brief period, such as an hour at a weekend church service. What do you think sustains wild gratitude toward Jesus day after day?

FOR DEEPER STUDY

A similar event is recorded in Luke 7:36–50. How was this event like and unlike what Mary did in Bethany? Why do you suppose women responded to Jesus like this?

In Ephesians 1:3–14, Paul praises God for a whole list of things God has done for us through Christ. For which ones are you deeply grateful, and which ones do you perhaps take for granted or just not understand?

DEVELOPING YOUR GIFTS FOR SERVICE   20 min.

13. Plan an extended time of worship for your group. If weather permits, consider an outdoor field trip to a park or even to the mountains, ocean, lake, or forest. Alternatively, have an evening devoted completely to worship. Ideas for planning an extended worship experience are on pages 92–93. Which two group members are willing to plan this event?

SURRENDERING YOUR LIFE FOR GOD'S PLEASURE   15–30 min.

14. How can the group pray for you this week?

15. Close your meeting with some extravagant worship that expresses wild gratitude to God. What seems extravagant to your group? Some ideas:

☐ Dancing and singing
☐ Praying on your knees
☐ Taping up some poster paper and letting group members write their thanks to God with colored markers

STUDY NOTES

Passover (John 12:1). Passover commemorated the night God freed Israel from Egypt (Exodus 12). Jewish males who were thirteen years or older were supposed to go to Jerusalem for Passover. By the time of Jesus, many Jews lived hundreds of miles from Jerusalem, so not all could go there every year. Still, "Jews from all over the Roman Empire would converge on Jerusalem to celebrate.... For this holiday, Jerusalem, a town of about 50,000, swelled to 250,000 people."[2] Tempers were hot, and the Roman army was out in force to prevent the Jews from rioting.

Pure nard (12:3). Ancient people believed that anointing oils and ointments could "penetrate deep into the body and impart

---

[2]"John," The Life Application Commentary Series CD-ROM, © 1997, 1998, 1999 and 2000 by the Livingstone Corporation. Produced with permission of Tyndale House Publishers, Inc.

strength, health, beauty and even joy."[3] The Jews anointed persons to soften skin, heal the sick, welcome a guest, honor the dead, coronate kings, and consecrate priests. Instead of pouring a little perfumed oil on a guest's head, Mary used a whole pint of extremely costly ointment. Jesus said she foresaw his coming need to be anointed for burial (John 12:7; compare 19:38–40). None of the other disciples seems to have come to grips with Jesus' prediction of his impending death.

[3]W. Brunotte, "Anoint," *The New International Dictionary of New Testament Theology*, CD-ROM version (Grand Rapids: Zondervan, 1999).

PRAYER AND PRAISE REPORT

Briefly share your prayer requests with the large group, making notations below. Then gather in smaller groups of two to four to pray for each other.

Date: _____

Prayer Requests

_____
_____
_____
_____
_____
_____
_____
_____
_____
_____

Praise Report

_____
_____
_____
_____
_____
_____
_____
_____
_____
_____
_____

REFLECTIONS

Use this page to write out your prayers, your thoughts about your daily Bible reading, or your meditations on a verse from the passage you have already studied. Below are some suggested verses for meditation. The Bible Reading Plans are on pages 85–86.

For Meditation: Mark 14:3 or 14:6–9

DVD NOTES

If you are watching the accompanying *Surrendering to Christ Together* DVD, write down what you sense God saying to you through the speaker. (If you'd like to hear a sample of the DVD teaching segment, go to www.lifeto-gether.com/ExperiencingChristTogether.)

_____

_____

_____

_____

_____

_____

_____

_____

_____

_____

_____

_____

_____

_____

_____

_____

_____

_____

_____

_____

_____

_____

ULTIMATE TRUST

For six months, Michelle and Julian—a churchgoing, unmarried Christian couple—were periodically sleeping together.

Michelle's blush and downcast eyes told how it felt to admit this to her women's group. "Julian said he accepted Christ last year," she explained, "but I still feel pressure to sleep with him. He knows how badly I feel later and that God doesn't want us to be sexually active. I don't know what to do."

Laura and Jill didn't know how to respond. The three unmarried women discussed God's call for sexual purity and prayed that Michelle would stand firm throughout the week. At their next group meeting Michelle confessed, "We failed again."

As Laura and Jill learned more about Julian, it became apparent that his faith was uncertain. Michelle described him as "spiritually dead."

"If Julian's heart isn't willing to change, then maybe the only thing you can do is leave the relationship." Laura and Jill agreed on the very thing Michelle didn't want to hear. She envisioned herself hopelessly alone—her worst nightmare. She decided to give Julian another chance.

But weeks passed, and the sexual battle persisted. As Michelle's guilt increased, she began to resent Julian. She vowed to end the relationship. Three days passed, and she was still unable to do it. On the fourth day, Laura called Michelle. "God wants something better for you. It may not be what you expect, and I know how scared you are to be alone, but in his goodness he will provide." Later that evening, Michelle broke up with Julian.

Today, though thirty-three and single, Michelle believes that God is good and that no matter her future, she made the right choice.

CONNECTING WITH GOD'S FAMILY   10 min.

Have someone open the group in prayer and then spend a brief time of worship using the LIFE TOGETHER Worship Series or another worship CD. Reflect on a time when you surrendered to God something or someone that you held dear. Then connect either as a whole group (question 1) or as spiritual partners (question 2).

1. If you could ask God one question today, what would it be?

   Or,

2. Sit with your spiritual partner and look at your health plan. What has been happening in the area in which you decided to surrender yourself to God? What has God been saying in your personal time with him?

GROWING TO BE LIKE CHRIST   40 min.

When Mary poured perfumed oil on Jesus, he said she was anointing his body for burial. He knew he'd be arrested and executed within a few days. Sure enough, barely two days later found him in a garden outside Jerusalem, waiting for the arresting soldiers to arrive. And knowing it had to be this way didn't make it easy. He trusted his Father's wisdom, yet his emotions were fully human.

Few of us will ever face torture or death for our faith, but most of us will face moments when doing what God wants will feel agonizing. There are times when doing the right thing means venturing into the unknown, when doing God's will is costly. At those times, knowing Jesus has been there ahead of us can make a huge difference.

3. Read Mathew 26:36–46. What emotions does Jesus feel in this scene?

4. What does Jesus want from his friends in this dark hour?

5. Does it surprise you that Jesus is so honest with his friends about his feelings? Why or why not?

6. Study Jesus' prayers in verses 39 and 42. What strikes you as significant in what he asks for and what's important to him?

7. Why is it important to know that surrendering to the Father's will wasn't always easy for Jesus?

8. What do you think enabled Jesus to go through with what he had to do, despite his emotions? (You might look at Hebrews 12:2.)

FOR DEEPER STUDY

Read John 17:1–5. What priorities and convictions enabled Jesus to go through with a fearful ordeal?

Jesus quoted Psalm 22:1 on the cross. How does the psalmist deal with suffering and sorrow in Psalm 22?

Why do you think Ecclesiastes 7:3 says sorrow is better than laughter? When is sorrow good?

Examine the attitudes toward the Father that Jesus said should shape the way we pray (Matthew 7:7–12). How do you see these attitudes at work in Jesus' prayers, both in John 17 and in Matthew 26?

 SURRENDERING YOUR LIFE FOR GOD'S PLEASURE 15–30 min.

There are two kinds of surrender to the Father's will:

- *Passive surrender* is acceptance of what is—an illness, a job loss, a crisis with our children. We acknowledge painful emotions (sorrow, anger). We also let God take us through those emotions to a place where our mind, emotions, and will line up to accept the painful situation. We don't "give up" in the sense of despairing, ceasing to look for solutions, or ceasing to pray. Rather, we come to a place where we trust God to meet our deepest needs, whatever happens.
- *Active surrender* is the decision to take action in accord with what we believe God wants us to do, despite risks and costs. It often involves moving from a situation that feels relatively safe to one full of unknowns. It can be harder than passive surrender because we genuinely have the option of avoiding the tough situation. (It's easier to accept what we can't avoid than to accept what we can avoid.) In Gethsemane, Jesus surrendered actively to the Father's will. He could have avoided the cross, but he chose not to.

These categories aren't rigid. For example, accepting a job loss leads to actively searching for a new job. Accepting a teenager's crisis also involves actively responding. Still, it's helpful to know the difference between accepting what happens to us in the natural course of life and embracing some initiative God wants us to take.

9. Is God calling you to any active surrender? If so, what is it? How have you responded so far?

10. Is God calling you to any passive surrender? If so, what do you need to accept?

11. Pray for the people who shared answers to questions 9 and 10.

SHARING YOUR LIFE MISSION EVERY DAY   10 min.

Every Christian is called to join in reproducing Christ's life in others over time. Sometimes God calls us to help another person one-on-one. Sometimes we reach out as couples or as a group. Some of us are called to become shepherds of small groups. Consider the following two ways of surrendering to God what you've been learning in this group:

12. The Father often places someone in our life who needs our help to know him better. Yet we're often unwilling to take the time to reach out. Is there an unbeliever in your life with whom the Father wants you to spend some time? What about a believer who could benefit from what you've been learning in this study? You could do this study again, one-on-one, with that person. Ask the Lord to bring a name to mind, and if one comes to you, write it down.

13. Would you be willing to take a six-week break from this group to lead a new group through this study or another in the EXPERIENCING CHRIST TOGETHER series? During that time, you can coach one of the new group's members to take over leadership. After six weeks, return to your current group. Maybe there are two people in your group willing to surrender the group for six weeks to help another group get started. Or maybe all of you want to go out in pairs to launch new groups for six weeks! Please prayerfully consider what God might want you to do.

STUDY NOTES

Sorrowful and troubled (Matthew 26:37). These words indicate deep grief, distress, heaviness of heart. Jesus had the normal human response to the ordeal ahead. He took that human response to the Father and submitted his will to him. Earlier he had said, "What shall I say? 'Father, save me from this hour?' No, it was for this very reason I came to this hour. Father, glorify your name" (John 12:27–28). Jesus was committed to doing whatever would bring glory to the Father.

Cup (26:39). In the Old Testament, God's cup is a reference to his judgment, his holy hatred of sin (Psalm 75:8; Isaiah 51:17, 22; Jeremiah 25:15). Our sins aren't just unfortunate habits; they display rejection of God's goodness, and they harm the people and things he loves. Jesus took on the full guilt of our sin (2 Corinthians 5:21) and drank the cup of the Father's hatred of sin to the bottom. This was the fate that agonized Jesus in Gethsemane. He wasn't just afraid of torture and slow death. He dreaded becoming the embodiment of sin and the object of his beloved Father's hatred. But if he had said no, we would face that fate.

The spirit is willing, but the body is weak (26:41). The disciples had surrendered, but only up to the point where their bodies and instincts screamed, "No!" Jesus modeled for them how to withstand the instinct to flee pain. Prayer kept Jesus grounded in the Father. After his resurrection, his disciples learned to do the same.

PRAYER AND PRAISE REPORT

Briefly share your prayer requests with the large group, making notations below. Then gather in smaller groups of two to four to pray for each other.

Date: _____

Prayer Requests

_____

_____

_____

_____

_____

_____

_____

_____

_____

_____

Praise Report

_____

_____

_____

_____

_____

_____

_____

_____

_____

_____

REFLECTIONS

Use this page to write out your prayers, your thoughts about your daily Bible reading, or your meditations on a verse from the passage you have already studied. Below are some suggested verses for meditation. The Bible Reading Plans are on pages 85–86.

For Meditation: Matthew 26:38–39 or 26:42

DVD NOTES

If you are watching the accompanying *Surrendering to Christ Together* DVD, write down what you sense God saying to you through the speaker. (If you'd like to hear a sample of the DVD teaching segment, go to www.lifetogether.com/ExperiencingChristTogether.)

_____

_____

_____

_____

_____

_____

_____

_____

_____

_____

_____

_____

_____

_____

_____

_____

_____

_____

_____

_____

_____

_____

_____

_____

VICTORY OVER DEATH

You can tell a lot about a person by the way he dies.

Pablo Picasso, for example, was arguably the greatest painter of the twentieth century. He was perhaps the chief among a handful of artists who invented modern art. You might expect that he ended his life richly satisfied with his monumental accomplishment. He didn't. In fact, as his body began to give way to illness, he painted with more and more frenzy. In the face of death, all his previous work seemed futile, and he grew driven to paint *the* painting that would be his masterwork. He filled his house with paintings, but the more aware he was that they were not his best work, the more frantically he painted.

How different was the death of William Wilberforce in 1833. He had spent decades campaigning to abolish slavery in the British Empire, and even as his health failed, he continued to do everything he could. He hoped he would remain in his body long enough to see the slaves freed, but neither his letters nor his friends' comments reflect frenzy or anxiety. When the day finally came that Parliament outlawed slavery, Wilberforce thanked God with joy. Two days later his health failed rapidly, and on the following day he died.[4]

Wilberforce persevered because he had eternity in mind. Picasso was driven because what he saw as death's finality rendered his whole life futile. If we want to live with perseverance and joy rather than drivenness and despair, we have only to look into the eyes of the Lord who triumphed over death.

CONNECTING WITH GOD'S FAMILY   10 min.

1. If you knew you were going to die one year from today, how would you live that final year?

   Or,

---

[4]The contrast between Picasso and Wilberforce is noted by Os Guinness in *Entrepreneurs of Life: Faith and the Venture of Purposeful Living* (Colorado Springs: NavPress, 2001), 204–13.

2. Meet with your spiritual partner. What is the most valuable thing you have gained from having a spiritual partner and spending consistent personal time with God?

GROWING TO BE LIKE CHRIST   40 min.

The heart of Christian faith is that Christ was raised from the dead. During his earthly ministry, Jesus predicted that the authorities would kill him and that he would be resurrected (Mark 10:32–34). His resurrection proved the truth of everything he had said and done. Many of Jesus' followers faced torture and execution with the faith that he had defeated death.

We worship a crucified Lord who died to free us from sin. We also worship a resurrected and living Lord. Total surrender is safe, because he is alive and we too will live forever.

3. Read Matthew 28:1–10. If you were one of the women in this scene, what would you have seen?

What would you have heard?

What would you have thought and felt?

4. Read Matthew 28:11–15, and review 28:2–4. Why didn't the guards make public what they saw at the tomb?

5. If you were an ordinary person in Jerusalem at that time, and you heard both the women's version and the guards' revised version of what happened at the tomb, what would you have believed about this event? Why?

6. Matthew 28:16–20 illustrates how Jesus wanted his disciples to respond to his resurrection. How is each of the following relevant to your life as an individual and as a group?

☐ Trusting that he has all authority in heaven and on earth (verse 18)

☐ Helping people from all nations become Jesus' disciples (verse 19)

☐ Baptizing disciples in the name of the Father, the Son, and the Holy Spirit (verse 19)

☐ Teaching others, by your words and example, to obey everything Jesus commanded (verse 20)

☐ Trusting that Jesus is with you always (verse 20)

7. Jesus' resurrection frees you from fear of death, because it secures your eternal life (Hebrews 2:14–15; 1 Corinthians 15:54–58). Today is part of forever, the first day of eternity. Imagine that you really, really know you're going to live forever. That health problems and disability are temporary. That failure isn't final. How would that affect the way you live now—especially your willingness to surrender completely?

FOR DEEPER STUDY

What does Paul say the resurrection demonstrates in Romans 1:4? How does that fact affect you personally?

Why does Jesus' resurrection free you from having to fear death (Hebrews 2:14–15; 1 Corinthians 15:54–58)?

How is the Christian belief in bodily resurrection different from the belief that souls are immortal (1 Corinthians 15:35–54)? How is it different from reincarnation? Why does it matter that Jesus was raised bodily and didn't just return as a spirit?

How does Christ's resurrection affect your relationship to sin (Romans 6:1–14)? How should this affect your daily choices?

SHARING YOUR LIFE MISSION EVERY DAY   15–20 min.

8. What's next for your group? We encourage you to surrender your group to the Lord in one of these ways:

    ☐ Take a six-week break to launch one or more new groups (see question 13 of session 5)
    ☐ Focus your group outward by studying either *Serving Like Christ Together* or *Sharing Christ Together* in this series, if you haven't already.

9. This final session is a time to celebrate where you've been together and where you're going. Here are some things to celebrate:

   ☐ Have you surrendered yourself to God more deeply in some area as a result of this group? If so, share as much about that with the group as you are willing to share.

   ☐ Look at your Prayer and Praise Report. What answers to prayer have you received?

   ☐ Are any group members taking a break to help another group get started? If so, tell the group your greatest hope and your greatest fear.

   Gather around those who are going out to launch new groups and pray for them, especially in the area of their greatest fears. Give thanks for answered prayers and for the growth you've experienced in this study. Have a special time of worshiping your resurrected Lord and immersing yourselves in his presence.

10. Communion, or the Lord's Supper, is something Christians do to remember and honor what Jesus did for us through his death on the cross. How does your church celebrate Communion? Consider planning a time to share Communion together. Ask your pastor for guidance, and see www.lifetogether.com for a free download of instructions for sharing Communion as a small group.

11. Allow those who are planning your worship field trip or event to update the group on the plan.

STUDY NOTES

Guards (Matthew 28:4). The authorities had placed Roman guards at the tomb to make sure nobody stole the body and claimed Jesus had risen (27:62–66).

Baptizing them in the name of (28:19). "The *name*, in the biblical world, is never just words, but involves the thing named."[5] Jesus established baptism in water as a rite of passage that represented a change in the baptized person's identity. The person symbolically died and was reborn as a child of the Father, disciple of the Son, and bearer of the Holy Spirit. Being lowered in the water of baptism identified the believer with Christ's death; rising from the water identified him with Christ's resurrection (Romans 6:3–4). This was not supposed to be a ritual done and then forgotten. Believers were supposed to remember their new identity and live accordingly.

[5]Dallas Willard, *Renovation of the Heart* (Colorado Springs: NavPress, 2002), 267.

PRAYER AND PRAISE REPORT

Briefly share your prayer requests with the large group, making notations below. Then gather in smaller groups of two to four to pray for each other.

Date: _____

Prayer Requests

_____

_____

_____

_____

_____

_____

_____

_____

_____

_____

Praise Report

_____

_____

_____

_____

_____

_____

_____

_____

_____

_____

REFLECTIONS

Use this page to write out your prayers, your thoughts about your daily Bible reading, or your meditations on a verse from the passage you have already studied. Below are some suggested verses for meditation. The Bible Reading Plans are on pages 85–86.

For Meditation: Matthew 28:5–6 or 28:18–20

DVD NOTES

If you are watching the accompanying *Surrendering to Christ Together* DVD, write down what you sense God saying to you through the speaker. (If you'd like to hear a sample of the DVD teaching segment, go to www.lifeto-gether.com/ExperiencingChristTogether.)

_____

_____

_____

_____

_____

_____

_____

_____

_____

_____

_____

_____

_____

_____

_____

_____

_____

_____

_____

_____

_____

_____

_____

_____

_____

_____

FREQUENTLY ASKED QUESTIONS

What do we do on the first night of our group?

Like all fun things in life—have a party! A "get to know you" coffee, dinner, or dessert is a great way to launch a new study. You may want to review the LIFE TOGETHER Agreement (pages 72–73) and share the names of a few friends you can invite to join you. But most importantly, have fun before your study time begins.

Where do we find new members for our group?

This can be troubling, especially for new groups that have only a few people or for existing groups that lose a few people along the way. We encourage you to pray with your group and then brainstorm a list of people from work, church, your neighborhood, your children's school, family, the gym, and so forth. Then have each group member invite several of the people on his or her list. Another good strategy is to ask church leaders to make an announcement or allow a bulletin insert.

No matter how you find members, it's vital that you stay on the lookout for new people to join your group. All groups tend to go through healthy attrition—the result of moves, releasing new leaders, ministry opportunities, and so forth—and if the group gets too small, it could be at risk of shutting down. If you and your group stay open, you'll be amazed at the people God sends your way. The next person just might become a friend for life. You never know!

How long will this group meet?

It's totally up to the group—once you come to the end of this six-week study. Most groups meet weekly for at least the first six weeks, but every other week can work as well. We strongly recommend that the group meet for the first six months on a weekly basis if at all possible. This allows for continuity, and if people miss a meeting they aren't gone for a whole month.

At the end of this study, each group member may decide if he or she wants to continue on for another six-week study. Some groups launch relationships for years to come, and others are stepping-stones into another group experience. Either way, enjoy the journey.

Can we do this study on our own?

Absolutely! This may sound crazy but one of the best ways to do this study is not with a full house but with a few friends. You may choose to gather with one other couple who would enjoy going to the movies or having a quiet dinner and then walking through this study. Jesus will be with you even if there are only two of you (Matthew 18:20).

What if this group is not working for us?

You're not alone! This could be the result of a personality conflict, life stage difference, geographical distance, level of spiritual maturity, or any number of things. Relax. Pray for God's direction, and at the end of this six-week study, decide whether to continue with this group or find another. You don't buy the first car you look at or marry the first person you date, and the same goes with a group. Don't bail out before the six weeks are up—God might have something to teach you. Also, don't run from conflict or prejudge people before you have given them a chance. God is still working in you too!

Who is the leader?

Most groups have an official leader. But ideally, the group will mature and members will rotate the leadership of meetings. We have discovered that healthy groups rotate hosts/leaders and homes on a regular basis. This model ensures that all members grow, give their unique contribution, and develop their gifts. This study guide and the Holy Spirit can keep things on track even when you rotate leaders. Christ has promised to be in your midst as you gather. Ultimately, God is your leader each step of the way.

How do we handle the child care needs in our group?

Very carefully. Seriously, this can be a sensitive issue. We suggest that you empower the group to openly brainstorm solutions. You may try one option that works for a while and then adjust over time. Our favorite approach is for adults to meet in the living room or dining room, and to share the cost of a babysitter (or two) who can be with the kids in a different part of the house. In this way, parents don't have to be away from their children all evening when their children are too young to be left at home. A second option is to use one home for the kids and a second home (close by or a phone call away) for the adults. A third idea is to rotate the responsibility of providing a lesson or care for the children either in the same home or in another home nearby. This can be an incredible blessing for kids. Finally, the most common idea is to decide that you need to have a night to invest in your spiritual lives individually or as a couple, and to make your own arrangements for child care. No matter what decision the group makes, the best approach is to dialogue openly about both the problem and the solution.

To answer your further questions, we have created a website called www.lifetogether.com/ExperiencingChristTogether that can be your small group coach. Here are ten reasons to check out this website:

1. Top twenty questions every new leader asks
2. Common problems most new leaders face and ways to overcome them
3. Seven steps to building a healthy small group in six weeks
4. Free downloadable resources and leadership support
5. Additional leadership training material for every lesson in the EXPERIENCING CHRIST TOGETHER series
6. Ten stories from leaders who successfully completed this study
7. Free chat rooms and bulletin boards
8. Downloadable Health Assessments and Health Plans for individuals or groups
9. A chance to join a community of small group leaders by affinity, geography, or denominational affiliation
10. Best of all, a free newsletter with the best ideas from leaders around the world

LIFE TOGETHER AGREEMENT

OUR PURPOSE

To transform our spiritual lives by cultivating our spiritual health in a healthy small group community. In addition, we: _____

_____

_____.

OUR VALUES

Group Attendance	To give priority to the group meeting. We will call or email if we will be late or absent. (Completing the Small Group Calendar on page 74 will minimize this issue.)
Safe Environment	To help create a safe place where people can be heard and feel loved. (Please, no quick answers, snap judgments, or simple fixes.)
Respect Differences	To be gentle and gracious to people with different spiritual maturity, personal opinions, temperaments, or imperfections. We are all works in progress.
Confidentiality	To keep anything that is shared strictly confidential and within the group, and to avoid sharing improper information about those outside the group.
Encouragement for Growth	To be not just takers but givers of life. We want to spiritually multiply our life by serving others with our God-given gifts.
Welcome for Newcomers	To keep an open chair and share Jesus' dream of finding a shepherd for every sheep.
Shared Ownership	To remember that every member is a minister and to ensure that each attender will share a

	small team role or responsibility over time. (See Team Roles on pages 75–77.)
Rotating Hosts/Leaders and Homes	To encourage different people to host the group in their homes, and to rotate the responsibility of facilitating each meeting. (See the Small Group Calendar on page 74.)

OUR EXPECTATIONS

- Refreshments/mealtimes _____

- Child care _____

- When we will meet (day of week) _____

- Where we will meet (place) _____

- We will begin at (time)_____ and end at _____

- We will do our best to have some or all of us attend a worship service together. Our primary worship service time will be _____

- Date of this agreement _____

- Date we will review this agreement again _____

- Who (other than the leader) will review this agreement at the end of this study_____

SMALL GROUP CALENDAR

Planning and calendaring can help ensure the greatest participation at every meeting. At the end of each meeting, review this calendar. Be sure to include a regular rotation of host homes and leaders, and don't forget birthdays, socials, church events, holidays, and mission/ministry projects. Go to www.lifetogether.com for an electronic copy of this form and more than a hundred ideas for your group to do together.

Date	Lesson	Host Home	Dessert/Meal	Leader
Monday, January 15	1	Steve and Laura's	Joe	Bill

TEAM ROLES

The Bible makes clear that every member, not just the small group leader, is a minister in the body of Christ. In a healthy small group, every member takes on some small role or responsibility. It's more fun and effective if you team up on these roles.

Review the team roles and responsibilities below, and have each member volunteer for a role or participate on a team. If someone doesn't know where to serve or is holding back, have the group suggest a team or role. It's best to have one or two people on each team so you have each of the five purposes covered. Serving in even a small capacity will not only help your leader but also will make the group more fun for everyone. Don't hold back. Join a team!

The opportunities below are broken down by the five purposes and then by a *crawl* (beginning step), *walk* (intermediate step), or *run* (advanced step). Try to cover at least the crawl and walk roles, and select a role that matches your group, your gifts, and your maturity. If you can't find a good step or just want to see other ideas, go to www.lifetogether.com and see what other groups are choosing.

Team Roles	Team Player(s)

CONNECTING TEAM (Fellowship and Community Building)

Crawl: Host a social event or group activity in the first week or two. _____

Walk: Create a list of uncommitted members and then invite them to an open house or group social. _____

Run: Plan a twenty-four-hour retreat or weekend getaway for the group. Lead the Connecting time each week for the group. _____

GROWING TEAM (Discipleship and Spiritual Growth)

Crawl: Coordinate the spiritual partners for the
group. Facilitate a three- or four-person
discussion circle during the Bible study
portion of your meeting. Coordinate the
discussion circles.

_____
_____

Walk: Tabulate the Personal Health Assessments
and Health Plans in a summary to let
people know how you're doing as a group.
Encourage personal devotions through group discussions
and pairing up with spiritual (accountability) partners.

_____
_____

Run: Take the group on a prayer walk, or plan
a day of solitude, fasting, or personal retreat.

_____
_____

SERVING TEAM (Discovering Your God-Given Design for Ministry)

Crawl: Ensure that every member finds a
group role or team he or she enjoys.

_____
_____

Walk: Have every member take a gift test
(see www.lifetogether.com) and
determine your group's gifts. Plan a
ministry project together.

_____
_____

Run: Help each member decide on a
way to use his or her unique gifts
somewhere in the church.

_____
_____

SHARING TEAM (Sharing and Evangelism)

Crawl: Coordinate the group's Prayer and
Praise Report of friends and family
who don't know Christ.

_____
_____

Walk: Search for group mission opportunities
and plan a cross-cultural group activity.

_____
_____

Run: Take a small-group "vacation" to host a
six-week group in your neighborhood
or office. Then come back together
with your current group.

_____
_____

SURRENDERING TEAM (Surrendering Your Heart to Worship)

Crawl: Maintain the group's Prayer
and Praise Report or journal.

_____

_____

Walk: Lead a brief time of worship each
week (at the beginning or end of
your meeting), either a cappella or
using a song from the DVD or the
LIFE TOGETHER Worship DVD/CD.

_____

_____

Run: Plan a unique time of worship through
Communion, foot washing, night of
prayer, or nature walking.

_____

_____

PERSONAL HEALTH ASSESSMENT

CONNECTING WITH GOD AND OTHERS

	Just Beginning	Getting Going	Well Developed
I am deepening my understanding of and friendship with God in community with others.	1 2 3 4 5		
I am growing in my ability both to share and to show my love to others.	1 2 3 4 5		
I am willing to share my real needs for prayer and support from others.	1 2 3 4 5		
I am resolving conflict constructively and am willing to forgive others.	1 2 3 4 5		

CONNECTING Total _____

GROWING IN YOUR SPIRITUAL JOURNEY

I have a growing relationship with God through regular
    time in the Bible and in prayer (spiritual habits). 1 2 3 4 5

I am experiencing more of the characteristics of
    Jesus Christ (love, patience, gentleness, courage,
    self-control, and so forth) in my life. 1 2 3 4 5

I am avoiding addictive behaviors (food, television,
    busyness, and the like) to meet my needs. 1 2 3 4 5

I am spending time with a Christian friend (spiritual partner)
    who celebrates and challenges my spiritual growth. 1 2 3 4 5

GROWING Total _____

SERVING WITH YOUR GOD-GIVEN DESIGN

I have discovered and am further developing my
    unique God-given design. 1 2 3 4 5

I am regularly praying for God to show me
    opportunities to serve him and others. 1 2 3 4 5

I am serving in a regular (once a month or more)
    ministry in the church or community. 1 2 3 4 5

I am a team player in my small group by sharing
    some group role or responsibility. 1 2 3 4 5

SERVING Total _____

| | Just Beginning | Getting Going | Well Developed |

SHARING GOD'S LOVE IN EVERYDAY LIFE

I am cultivating relationships with non-Christians and praying for God to give me natural opportunities to share his love.   1 2 3 4 5

I am praying and learning about where God can use me and my group cross-culturally for missions.   1 2 3 4 5

I am investing my time in another person or group who needs to know Christ.   1 2 3 4 5

I am regularly inviting unchurched or unconnected friends to my church or small group.   1 2 3 4 5

SHARING Total _____

SURRENDERING YOUR LIFE TO GOD

I am experiencing more of the presence and power of God in my everyday life.   1 2 3 4 5

I am faithfully attending services and my small group to worship God.   1 2 3 4 5

I am seeking to please God by surrendering every area of my life (health, decisions, finances, relationships, future, and the like) to him.   1 2 3 4 5

I am accepting the things I cannot change and becoming increasingly grateful for the life I've been given.   1 2 3 4 5

SURRENDERING Total _____

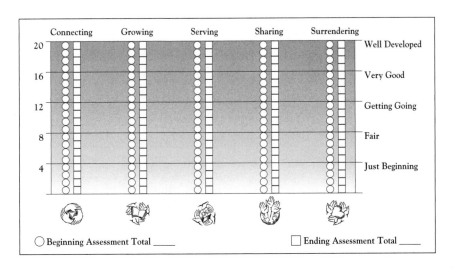

PERSONAL HEALTH PLAN

This worksheet could become your single most important feature in this study. On it you can record your personal priorities before the Father. It will help you live a healthy spiritual life, balancing all five of God's purposes.

PURPOSE	PLAN
CONNECT	WHO are you connecting with spiritually?
GROW	WHAT is your next step for growth?
DEVELOP	WHERE are you serving?
SHARE	WHEN are you shepherding another in Christ?
SURRENDER	HOW are you surrendering your heart?

Additional copies of the Personal Health Plan may be downloaded in a larger format at www.lifetogether.com/healthplan.

DATE	MY PROGRESS	PARTNER'S PROGRESS

SAMPLE PERSONAL HEALTH PLAN

This worksheet could become your single most important feature in this study. On it you can record your personal priorities before the Father. It will help you live a healthy spiritual life, balancing all five of God's purposes.

PURPOSE	PLAN
CONNECT	WHO are you connecting with spiritually? *Bill and I will meet weekly by email or phone.*
GROW	WHAT is your next step for growth? *Regular devotions or journaling my prayers 2x/week*
DEVELOP	WHERE are you serving? *Serving in Children's Ministry* *Go through GIFTS class*
SHARE	WHEN are you shepherding another in Christ? *Shepherding Bill at lunch or hosting a starter group in the fall*
SURRENDER	HOW are you surrendering your heart? *Help with our teenager* *New job situation*

DATE	MY PROGRESS	PARTNER'S PROGRESS
3/5	Talked during our group	Figured out our goals together
3/12	Missed our time together	Missed our time together
3/26	Met for coffee and review of my goals	Met for coffee
4/10	Emailed prayer requests	Bill sent me his prayer requests
3/5	Great start on personal journaling	Read Mark 1–6 in one sitting!
3/12	Traveled and not doing well this week	Journaled about Christ as Healer
3/26	Back on track	Busy and distracted; asked for prayer
3/1	Need to call Children's Pastor	
3/26	Group did a serving project together	Agreed to lead group worship
3/30	Regularly rotating leadership	Led group worship—great job!
3/5	Called Jim to see if he's open to joining our group	Wanted to invite somebody, but didn't
3/12	Preparing to start a group this fall	
3/30	Group prayed for me	Told friend something he's learning about Christ
3/5	Overwhelmed but encouraged	Scared to lead worship
3/15	Felt heard and more settled	Issue with wife
3/30	Read book on teens	Glad he took on his fear

JOURNALING 101

Henri Nouwen says effective and lasting ministry *for* God grows out of a quiet place alone *with* God. This is why journaling is so important.

The greatest adventure of our lives is found in the daily pursuit of knowing, growing in, serving, sharing, and worshiping Christ forever. This is the essence of a purposeful life: to see all five biblical purposes fully formed and balanced in our lives. Only then are we "complete in Christ" (Colossians 1:28, NASB).

David poured his heart out to God by writing psalms. The book of Psalms contains many of his honest conversations with God in written form, including expressions of every imaginable emotion on every aspect of his life. Like David, we encourage you to select a strategy to integrate God's Word and journaling into your devotional time. Use any of the following resources:

- Bible
- One-year Bible
- New Testament Bible Challenge Reading Plan (www.lifetogether.com/readingprograms)
- Devotional book
- Topical Bible study plan

Before or after you read a portion of God's Word, speak to God in honest reflection or response in the form of a written prayer. You may begin this time by simply finishing the sentence "Father . . . ," "Yesterday Lord . . . ,"or "Thank you, God, for. . . ." Share with him where you are at the present moment; express your hurts, disappointments, frustrations, blessings, victories, gratefulness. Whatever you do with your journal, make a plan that fits you so you'll have a positive experience. Consider sharing highlights of your progress and experiences with some or all of your group members, especially your spiritual partner(s). You may find they want to join and even encourage you in this journey. Most of all, enjoy the ride and cultivate a more authentic, growing walk with God.

BIBLE READING PLANS

Plan A: 30 Days through the Gospel of John

Imagine sitting at the feet of Jesus himself: the Teacher who knows how to live life well, the Savior who died for you, the Lord who commands the universe. Like his first disciples, you can follow him around, watch what he does, listen to what he says, and pattern your life after his.

Find a quiet place, and have ready a notebook or journal in which you can write what you learn and what you want to say back to God. You may also use the Reflections pages at the end of each session of this study.

As you read, ask yourself:

• What in this passage convinces me to entrust myself completely to Jesus?

• What about him moves me to worship?

☐ Day 1   John 1:1–18
☐ Day 2   John 1:19–51
☐ Day 3   John 2:1–11
☐ Day 4   John 2:12–25
☐ Day 5   John 3:1–21
☐ Day 6   John 3:22–36
☐ Day 7   John 4
☐ Day 8   John 5:1–15
☐ Day 9   John 5:16–47
☐ Day 10 John 6:1–24
☐ Day 11 John 6:25–71
☐ Day 12 John 7:1–24
☐ Day 13 John 7:25–53
☐ Day 14 John 8:1–30
☐ Day 15 John 8:31–59

☐ Day 16 John 9
☐ Day 17 John 10
☐ Day 18 John 11
☐ Day 19 John 12
☐ Day 20 John 13
☐ Day 21 John 14:1–14
☐ Day 22 John 14:15–31
☐ Day 23 John 15:1–17
☐ Day 24 John 15:18–27
☐ Day 25 John 16
☐ Day 26 John 17
☐ Day 27 John 18
☐ Day 28 John 19
☐ Day 29 John 20
☐ Day 30 John 21

Plan B: 30 Days through the Psalms

If you've read John recently, you may prefer to read Psalms each day. Below is a plan to read five psalms per day for a month, but you may read fewer if you want to linger over them. As you read, ask yourself:

• What in this psalm convinces me to entrust myself completely to God?

• What in this psalm moves me to worship?

☐	Day 1	Psalm 1–5	☐ Day 16	Psalm 76–80
☐	Day 2	Psalm 6–10	☐ Day 17	Psalm 81–85
☐	Day 3	Psalm 11–15	☐ Day 18	Psalm 86–90
☐	Day 4	Psalm 16–20	☐ Day 19	Psalm 91–95
☐	Day 5	Psalm 21–25	☐ Day 20	Psalm 96–100
☐	Day 6	Psalm 26–30	☐ Day 21	Psalm 101–105
☐	Day 7	Psalm 31–35	☐ Day 22	Psalm 106–110
☐	Day 8	Psalm 36–40	☐ Day 23	Psalm 111–115
☐	Day 9	Psalm 41–45	☐ Day 24	Psalm 116–120
☐	Day 10	Psalm 46–50	☐ Day 25	Psalm 121–125
☐	Day 11	Psalm 51–55	☐ Day 26	Psalm 126–130
☐	Day 12	Psalm 56–60	☐ Day 27	Psalm 131–135
☐	Day 13	Psalm 61–65	☐ Day 28	Psalm 136–140
☐	Day 14	Psalm 66–70	☐ Day 29	Psalm 141–145
☐	Day 15	Psalm 71–75	☐ Day 30	Psalm 146–150

LEADING FOR
THE FIRST TIME

- **Sweaty palms are a healthy sign.** The Bible says God is gracious to the humble. Remember who is in control; the time to worry is when you're not worried. Those who are soft in heart (and sweaty-palmed) are those whom God is sure to speak through.

- **Seek support.** Ask your leader, coleader, or close friend to pray for you and prepare with you before the session. Walking through the study will help you anticipate potentially difficult questions and discussion topics.

- **Bring your uniqueness to the study.** Lean into who you are and how God wants you to uniquely lead the study.

- **Prepare. Prepare. Prepare.** Go through the session several times. If you are using the DVD, listen to the teaching segment and Leadership Lifter. Go to www.lifetogether.com and download pertinent files. Consider writing in a journal or fasting for a day to prepare yourself for what God wants to do.

- **Don't wait until the last minute to prepare.**

- **Ask for feedback so you can grow.** Perhaps in an email or on cards handed out at the study, have everyone write down three things you did well and one thing you could improve on. Don't get defensive, but show an openness to learn and grow.

- **Use online resources.** Go to www.lifetogether.com and listen to Brett Eastman share the weekly Leadership Lifter and download any additional notes or ideas for your session. You may also want to subscribe to the Doing Life Together Newsletter and LLT Newsletter. Both can be obtained for free by signing up at www.lifetogether.com/subscribe.

- **Prayerfully consider launching a new group.** This doesn't need to happen overnight, but God's heart is for this to happen over time. Not all

Christians are called to be leaders or teachers, but we are all called to be "shepherds" of a few someday.

- **Share with your group what God is doing in your heart**. God is searching for those whose hearts are fully his. Share your trials and victories. We promise that people will relate.

- **Prayerfully consider whom you would like to pass the baton to next week.** It's only fair. God is ready for the next member of your group to go on the faith journey you just traveled. Make it fun, and expect God to do the rest.

HOSTING AN OPEN HOUSE

If you're starting a new group, try planning an "open house" before your first formal group meeting. Even if you only have two to four core members, it's a great way to break the ice and to consider prayerfully who else might be open to join you over the next few weeks. You can also use this kick-off meeting to hand out study guides, spend some time getting to know each other, discuss each person's expectations for the group, and briefly pray for each other.

A simple meal or good desserts always make a kick-off meeting more fun. After people introduce themselves and share how they ended up being at the meeting (you can play a game to see who has the wildest story!), have everyone respond to a few icebreaker questions: "What is your favorite family vacation?" or "What is one thing you love about your church/our community?" or "What are three things about your life growing up that most people here don't know?" See www.lifetogether.com for more icebreaker ideas.

Next, ask everyone to tell what he or she hopes to get out of the study. You might want to review the LIFE TOGETHER Agreement (pages 72–73) and talk about each person's expectations and priorities.

Finally, set an open chair (maybe two) in the center of your group and explain that it represents someone who would enjoy or benefit from this group but who isn't here yet. Ask people to pray about whom they could invite to join the group over the next few weeks. Hand out postcards (see www.lifetogether.com for examples) and have everyone write an invitation or two. Don't worry about ending up with too many people—you can always have one discussion circle in the living room and another in the dining room after you watch the lesson. Each group could then report prayer requests and progress at the end of the session.

You can skip this kick-off meeting if your time is limited, but you'll experience a huge benefit if you take the time to connect with each other in this way.

Sunday school is one of the best places to begin building community in your church, and the EXPERIENCING CHRIST TOGETHER DVDs and study guides work in concert to help your Sunday school leadership team do it easily and effectively.

Each study guide of the LIFE TOGETHER curriculum includes a companion DVD with today's top Christian leaders speaking to the passage of Scripture under discussion. Here is one way to use the DVD in a Sunday school class:

- Moderator introduction: welcome the class, and read the Scripture passage for the session
- DVD teaching segment: ten to fifteen minutes
- Small group discussion: divide into small groups of eight to twelve and, using the questions from the curriculum, discuss how the passage applies to each person in the class

So often Sunday school consists of the star teacher with little involvement from others. To use the EXPERIENCING CHRIST TOGETHER DVDs effectively means recruiting a host of people to participate in the Sunday school program. We recommend four teams:

Moderators. These are the facilitators or leaders of the class. Their role is to transition the class through each step in the time together. For example, the moderator will welcome the class and open with prayer. In addition, he or she will introduce the DVD segment by reading the Scripture passage for the session. We recommend that you recruit several moderaters. That allows you to rotate the moderators each week. Doing so takes the pressure off people to commit to every week of the class—and it offers more people opportunity for upfront leadership. One church recruited three sets of moderators (a total of six) because the Sunday school leaders wanted to use the curriculum for twelve weeks. They knew that out of twelve weeks, one set of moderators would, likely, burn out; it's difficult for anyone to provide leadership for twelve straight weeks.

Discussion Guides. These are people who lead the follow-up discussion after the DVD teaching segment. If, for example, your Sunday school runs for an hour, you may want to plan on fifteen to twenty minutes for the DVD teaching segment and an additional twenty to thirty minutes in small group discussion afterward. One church recruited many of its seniors to lead the discussion groups. Some of them had felt excluded from ministry, and the role of discussion guide opened the door for them to serve.

Each discussion guide needs only to read through the passage and the questions in each study guide for preparation. After the DVD teaching segment, the moderator of the class asks the discussion guides to stand up. Then, people circle their chairs around each discussion guide. It's an easy way to create small groups each week. You may need to help some groups find more people or other groups to divide once more, if they end up too large. One church asked some of the discussion guides to move their groups into different rooms, because the seniors had a hard time hearing.

Hospitality Coordinators. These are those who oversee the food and drink for the class. Some classes may not provide this, but for those who do, it's important that multiple people join the team, so one or two people don't burn out over the course of the class.

Technical Coordinators. There's nothing worse than a DVD player that doesn't seem to work. Recruit at least one person to oversee making sure the DVD works each week. It's best, though, to recruit two or three people, in order to rotate them throughout the Sunday school series. It's important that the technical team has made sure the DVD player works *before* the class begins.

One church decided to gather all the adult Sunday school classes together for a twelve-week series using the LIFE TOGETHER DVD and study guides. What happened was amazing—instead of Sunday school starting off with 140 people and ending up with half that many at the end of the fall, attendance stayed high the entire time. Instead of one Sunday school class being led by one or two teachers, more than thirty-five people were involved in some kind of leadership—as moderators, discussion guides, hospitality (food) coordinators, or technical coordinators. The fifteen-minute time at the beginning of Sunday school for coffee and snacks (fruit, coffee cake, etc.) proved just as valuable as the content portion!

The fall program gave the church a new vision for how Sunday school can support the larger issue of spiritual formation and life change. For more ideas and practical tools to strengthen your small group ministry, go to www.lifetogethertoday.com.

A WORSHIP FIELD TRIP

Many people find that getting out of manmade structures and into the God-made natural world helps them renew their awareness of the Creator's presence. Where can you go for a worship field trip? Mountains, a forest, a lakeside, a park, and botanical gardens are all great options.

If weather makes an outdoor trip impossible, you can create an indoor environment for worship. One way is to darken the room and light lots of candles. An indoor environment also gives you access to electricity for a CD player.

Here are some things you can do on your field trip. Some require an outdoor setting, some require indoors, and some can work either way.

- [ ] Sing, perhaps with worship songs on a battery-powered CD player if you're outdoors.
- [ ] Take a slow, silent walk for at least half an hour. Pay attention to what you see, hear, and smell around you. Look for beauty that God has put into the world. When you note something beautiful, silently thank God for it. Afterward, talk about this experience with your group.
- [ ] Take half an hour alone to write a list of things for which you are thankful. Then gather as a group to offer your thanks to God. Read aloud some of what you've listed. You might take turns, each person thanking God for one thing at a time.
- [ ] Choose five of God's attributes. Have one person read aloud the first attribute, and then let everyone praise God for ways they've experienced that part of him. For example:

Wisdom
"Lord, I've seen your wisdom in . . ."
"Father, I know you're wise because . . ."

Some other attributes are holiness, majesty, power, kindness, mercy, justice, goodness, beauty, love, truth, omniscience (God knows everything), creation (God made everything), and omnipresence (God is everywhere).

☐ Sit and look at one thing God has made. It could be a landscape or a single object, such as a leaf or a shell. Really look at it. How does it reflect God's artistry or goodness or power or love? Reflect on this for fifteen minutes, then talk about your reflections with the group.

☐ Read a brief Bible passage on your own. Take fifteen to thirty minutes to write a prayer to God about what you've read. Afterward, read your prayer aloud in a time of group prayer if you feel comfortable doing so. Some possible passages are Exodus 34:4–7; Psalm 27; Psalm 131; Isaiah 6:1–7; Ephesians 1:3–10; and Philippians 2:5–11.

☐ Share the Lord's Supper (Communion) together.

INTRODUCTION

If your group is new, or even if you haven't been together for a few weeks, we recommend that you plan a kick-off meeting where you will pray, hand out study guides, spend some time getting to know each other, and discuss each person's expectations for the group. A meeting like this is a great way to start a group or step up people's commitments.

Most groups, if reconvened after a short break, will be renewed in seeing each other and open to increasing their commitment as much as 25 percent. We have seen some naturally move to a weekly format, begin doing homework, and commit to daily devotions simply because the leader shared his or her heart. What do you sense God wants from you and your group?

However, if your group is brand new, a simple meal, potluck, or even good desserts make a kick-off meeting more fun. After dessert, have everyone respond to an icebreaker question, such as, "How did you hear of this church, and what's one thing you love about it?" Or, "Tell us three things about your life growing up that most people here don't know."

Then ask everyone to tell what he or she hopes to get out of this study. You might want to review the LIFE TOGETHER Agreement (see pages 72–73) and talk about each person's expectations and priorities. You could discuss whether you want to do Bible study homework before each meeting—homework covering the questions under the Growing and/or the For Deeper Study sections. Review the Small Group Calendar on page 74 and talk about who else is willing to open their home or facilitate a meeting.

Finally, cast the vision, as Jesus did, to be inclusive not exclusive. Ask everyone to prayerfully think of people who would enjoy or benefit from a group like this. The beginning of a new study is a great time to welcome a few people into your circle. Have each person share a name or two and either make phone calls the coming week or handwrite invitations or postcards that very night. This will make it fun and also make it happen. At www.lifetogether.com we have a free email invitation you may send to every potential member. Don't worry about ending up with too many people—you can always have one discussion circle in the living room and another in the dining room.

SESSION ONE:
AFLOAT IN A STORM

As a leader, your most important job is to create an atmosphere where people are willing to talk honestly about what Christ's words and actions have to do with them. Especially if your group is new, be available before people arrive so you can greet them at the door. People are naturally nervous at a new group, so a hug or handshake can help put them at ease.

If your group is new and you aren't able to hold a get-to-know-you meeting before you launch into session 1, consider starting this first meeting half an hour early to give people time to socialize without shortchanging your time in the study. For example, you can have social time from 7:00 to 7:30, and by 7:40 you'll gather the group with a prayer. Even if only a few people are seated in the living room by 7:40, ask them to join you in praying for those who are coming and for God to be present among you as you meet. Others will notice you praying and will come and sit down. You may want to softly play music from the DVD or the Life Together Worship DVD/CD series as people arrive, and then turn up the volume when you are ready to begin. This first night will set the tone for the whole six weeks.

You may ask a few people to come early to help set up, pray, and introduce newcomers to others. Even if everyone is new, they don't know that yet and may be shy when they arrive. You might give people roles like setting up nametags or handing out drinks. This could be a great way to spot a coleader.

Question 1. You should be the first to answer this question while others are thinking about how to respond. You will set an example by being honest about how you really do deal with a crisis. Be sure to give everyone a chance to respond to this question, because it's a chance for the group to get to know each other. It's not necessary to go around the circle in order. Just ask for volunteers to respond.

Introduction to the Series. If this is your group's first Life Together study, take a moment after question 1 to orient the group to one principle that undergirds this series: *A healthy small group balances the purposes of the church.* Most small groups emphasize Bible study, fellowship, and prayer. But God has called us to reach out to others as well. He wants us to *do* what Jesus teaches, not just *learn about* it. You may spend less time in this series studying the Bible than some group members are used to. That's because you'll spend more time doing things the Bible says believers should do.

However, those who like more Bible study can find plenty of it in this series. At the end of each session, For Deeper Study provides more passages you can study on the same topic. If your group likes to do deeper Bible study, consider having members answer next week's Growing section questions ahead of time as homework. They can even study next week's For Deeper Study passages for homework too. Then, during the Growing portion of your meeting, you can share the high points of what you've learned.

If the five biblical purposes are new to your group, be sure to review them together on pages 8–10 of the Read Me First section.

Question 2. An agreement helps you clarify your group's priorities and cast new vision for what the group can be. Members can imagine what your group could be like if they lived these values. So turn to pages 72–73 and choose one value that you want to emphasize in this study. We've suggested some options. If you choose "spiritual partners," your group doesn't need to worry right now about what the partners will do. As leader, though, you might want to look ahead to session 2 to see how the partnerships work.

Question 3. Have someone read the Bible passage aloud. It's a good idea to ask someone ahead of time, because not everyone is comfortable reading aloud in public. When the passage has been read, ask question 3. *It is not necessary that everyone answer every question in the Bible study.* In fact, a group can become boring if you simply go around the circle and give answers. That is especially true with a question like this, whose purpose is simply to get all the facts on the table. Your goal is to create a discussion—which means that perhaps only a few people respond to each question and an engaging dialogue gets going. It's even fine to skip some questions in order to spend more time on questions you believe are most important.

Question 5. They should have trusted Jesus' words in verse 35 that he intended to get to the other side of the sea. They must have partially trusted that if they woke him, Jesus could do something about the storm, because they did wake him. But that wasn't enough faith, in Jesus' opinion, so he rebuked them.

Ironically, this is what most of us consider real faith: we hit a crisis and scream for Jesus' help. Isn't that better than trying to handle the crisis on our own? Yes, but to Jesus, that's not enough faith. We should at least trust him enough to dispense with the panicked feelings behind the prayer.

Some scholars even think Jesus expected his followers to trust that because they were his true followers, they had his authority to do what he did. That's a debatable position, but certainly we today have the Holy Spirit in us, so we have more authority to do God's work than we generally think we do. Enough to do miracles? Again, that's debatable, but those among us who walk most intimately with Christ do seem to have the Holy Spirit working through them in sometimes surprising ways.

Question 6. This question is also debatable. Should they have waited out the storm, trusting that they'd make it through because Jesus had said so? Should they have rebuked the storm in Jesus' name? Or should they have calmly wakened him and asked him to calm the storm?

Question 9. Fear and trust are automatic reactions rooted in deep beliefs. We may believe intellectually in Jesus' authority, while our ingrained habits of thought and feeling are rooted in the belief that we're on our own. To reframe our deep beliefs, we need to immerse ourselves in true thoughts about Christ. It's not enough to think true thoughts about God for an hour on Sunday and an hour in a midweek Bible study. We need to rehearse the truth about God over and over, all day long for an extended period of time.

Question 10. Let group members voice their confusion and pain. They need you to be the Good Shepherd's hands, eyes, and ears in this conversation. They need you to be sensitive and care about their pain. You don't need to solve their problems. You don't need to defend God or answer their questions and doubts. You just need to listen and care.

There are no quick fixes to complex problems. Minimizing someone's pain by trying to quickly solve it prevents you from communicating Christ's heart. God is very capable of healing someone's hurts. Try to avoid covering your awkwardness in the moment by filling it with words.

You may decide that someone's need is so important that the group should stop for a while and care for her. Or, you may decide after a few minutes to put a hand on someone's shoulder, pray briefly and compassionately for him, and let the group move on. It's okay if someone cries—just pass the tissues. Model Paul's teaching that we are to mourn with those who mourn (Romans 12:15). You can see why it might be a good time to gather in smaller (safer) circles for this discussion.

Your group members don't need you to lecture them about faith. They need you to demonstrate it by the way you deal with your own suffering, by your eagerness to spend personal time with God, and by the way you care for them when they're in pain.

Question 11. Be sure to save time to pray for each other. Some churches emphasize prayer for healing—if yours does, you can follow your church's practice in the way you approach this exercise. Other churches prefer to avoid a charismatic flavor in their small groups—if yours has that concern, you can pray for one another in whatever way seems comfortable. If you're concerned that some members might confuse or try to "fix" others through prayer, you can pray as a whole group and monitor how people pray. But don't be overly concerned: the very worst that will happen is that someone will pray in a way that distresses someone else, and if that happens you can simply talk to each person privately before your next meeting. As leader, you set the example of how people will pray for each other in your group, and most members will follow your lead.

Question 14. We've offered several options for personal time with God. Don't press seekers to do this, but every believer should have a plan for personal time with God. Walk the group through these options. If group members have never read through the Gospels (Matthew, Mark, Luke, and John), we strongly urge that they choose that option. This will immerse them in the person of Christ for the duration of this study.

For those who have done a lot of Bible study, we encourage the meditation option. Living with one short passage each week can help them move biblical truth from their heads into their hearts and actions. The prayer option—whether five minutes a day or thirty—is valuable for anyone. We strongly suggest that those who have never used a personal prayer journal give it a try.

Question 15. The "Circles of Life" is a vivid symbol of one of the values of the LIFE TOGETHER agreement: "welcome for newcomers." Some groups fear that newcomers will interrupt the intimacy that members have built over time. However, groups generally gain strength with the infusion of new blood. It's like a river of living water flowing into a stagnant pond. Some groups remain permanently open, while others open periodically, such as at the beginning and ending of a study. Love grows by giving itself away. If your circle becomes too large for easy face-to-face conversations, you can simply form a second discussion circle in another room of your home.

As leader, you should do this exercise yourself in advance and be ready to share the names of the people you're going to invite or connect with. Your modeling is the number-one example that people will follow. Give everyone a few moments in which to write down names before each shares. You might pray for a few of these names on the spot and/or later in the session. Encourage people not to be afraid to ask someone. Almost no one is annoyed to be invited to something! Most people are honored to be asked, even if they can't make it. You may want to distribute invitations and fill them out during the meeting. Check out the print and email invitations at www.lifetogether.com.

We encourage an outward focus for your group because groups that become too inwardly focused tend to become unhealthy over time. People naturally gravitate to feeding themselves through Bible study, prayer, and social time, so it's usually up to the leader to push them to consider how this inward nourishment can overflow into outward concern for others. Never forget: Jesus came to seek and save the lost and to find a shepherd for every sheep.

Question 1. Most groups share prayer requests and pray at the end of their meetings. This question is intended to expose your group to other prayer ideas. Consistency in a group is comforting and thus a strength, but groups need variety too or members become bored. If some group members are shy about praying aloud, don't force them. You may even ask two or three people beforehand if they're willing to get the ball rolling in this opening prayer time. If the group likes it, try it again from time to time.

Question 2. Jesus says a grain of wheat has to die to fulfill its purpose. That is, it's buried in the ground and lets its structure be so drastically altered that the grain ceases to exist as a grain. It now exists as something very different but very good: a stalk of wheat. Likewise, in order to accomplish his life purpose, Jesus had to die physically and be raised to life with a body that is very different from his old one, but very good.

Questions 4 and 5. Loving our life in this passage means making personal survival and advancement our top priority. Like Jesus, we need to be willing to risk everything we call "life" in order to fulfill our purpose. We need to be willing to have our deeply ingrained habits reshaped. We need to risk losing our most cherished goals. We may even need to be willing to give up our physical lives in his service, as countless martyrs have done. We may not have to give up all of this, but we need to be ready and willing to give up whatever is necessary. If we're not willing to have our selfish habits reshaped, we will remain their prisoners. If we're not willing to put God's goals ahead of our own, we won't have the time and energy to pursue the things for which God created us. If protecting ourselves is our top priority, we will end up with tiny, hard-shelled souls, like unsprouted kernels of wheat.

Because groups naturally dwell on personal growth and social time, you must emphasize fruitfulness, what they can give back to the world around them. Deep down, everybody wants to make an impact. They're just reluctant to sacrifice the things that get in the way of their making a difference. Help them identify the things they need to die to, such as TV, money, the size of their home, or perfect kids.

Question 6. We're limited. We each have finite time and energy. If we devote time and energy to loving others and nurturing Christ's life in their lives, that's time we're not devoting to our self-focused desires. That doesn't mean we shouldn't eat or sleep; it means that every act of love is to some degree an act of self-sacrifice.

Question 7. Jesus focused on the purpose of his life: to glorify the Father—that is, to reveal the Father's magnificence to everything that lives.

Question 10. You can break the ice by going first on this question. Most of us have some good goal that we treasure a bit more than we ought to, compared with the goals of loving God and others well. For instance, it's normal and good to want our children to become happy and successful, but some of us get a bit too much of our own egos wrapped up in our children's futures. That goal can limit our fruitfulness in love.

At the same time, it's important not to go to the opposite extreme and imagine that the "ordinary" things of life—career, family, and so on—don't really count for eternity, and that therefore most of what we devote the hours of our day to are almost worthless in God's sight. It does matter to God that we do good work in our careers, work that brings valuable products and services to people. Such work demonstrates fruitfulness. It does matter to God that we raise our children with love and justice, with their highest good and joy in mind. That's fruitfulness too. And God does want us to take joy in our day's labor (always understanding that in a fallen world, no work can be perfectly fulfilling all the time).

Question 11. For those who haven't done a LIFE TOGETHER study before, spiritual partners will be a new idea. We highly encourage you to try pairs or triplets for six weeks. It's so hard to start a spiritual practice such as prayer or consistent Bible reading with no support. A friend makes a huge difference. Partners can check in with each other weekly either at the beginning of your group meetings or outside the meeting.

Question 14. As leader, you're in the people development business. Part of your job is to help others discover and develop their gifts. You may not need their help to plan worship for your group, but they need you to let them take on a role and support them so that they succeed. Try to get at least two volunteers to team up to champion worship in your group. This will be an act of sacrificial love for the group that will bear much fruit. If no one volunteers, ask the group who they think would be good at it—someone who isn't already shouldering too much.

SESSION THREE:
TRUE GREATNESS

This session involves the positive side of surrender: pursuing God's will for your lives. Surrendering your futures to God not out of fear, but out of wanting to know what he wants.

Question 2. What John means in verse 23 is that his mission in life is to call people to prepare for Christ's arrival.

Question 3. John knew clearly that his mission wasn't about him; it was about Christ. He also knew he wasn't Christ, and said so. He said he wasn't even worthy to untie Christ's sandals—the task of a low slave. John was even reluctant to identify himself as the prophet like Elijah who would be Christ's official forerunner, even though Jesus later said that was exactly who John was (Matthew 11:14; 17:10–13; compare Malachi 4:5).

Questions 4 and 5. John's followers are competitive, wanting their ministry to be the biggest and most important. John rejoiced in Jesus becoming greater while he, John, became less important.

Question 8. Twenty minutes in pairs should give partners ten minutes each to talk about what God seems to be doing around them and how they might fit in. Some may have no idea how they could be involved in what God is doing, but their partners will see gifts in them that they could explore. They may even have ideas for ways their partner could serve God. Because this discussion could drag on, alert everyone at the halfway point so they can shift focus to the other partner, and then provide a one-minute notice at the end. If you have circles of three, they'll need to trim their sharing time accordingly. If you don't watch the clock, you'll never get back together to pray and worship.

Questions 1 and 2. Checking in with your spiritual partners (question 2) will be an option in all sessions from now on. You'll need to watch the clock and keep these conversations to ten minutes. If partners want more time together (as is ideal), they can connect before, after, or outside meetings. Give them a two-minute notice and hold to it if you ever want to get them back in the circle! If some group members are absent or newcomers have joined you, you may need to help partnerless people connect with new or temporary partners.

If you prefer, question 1 will always be a lighter icebreaker for the whole group. We encourage you, though, to let partners check in at least every other week so that those relationships grow solid. Please don't miss this opportunity to take your people deeper. Remember that the goal here is "transforming lives through community," and one-on-one time has an enormous return on time spent. In a week or two, you might want to ask the group how their partnerships are progressing. This will encourage those who are struggling to connect or accomplish their goals.

Question 3. The point of these questions is to get the facts on the table as quickly and simply as possible, so you can go on to discussing the meaning of the event. You definitely don't want to go around the circle and let everyone answer questions like these. One person can summarize the event, and one or two others can add important details that were missed.

Question 7. Mary was wildly grateful to Jesus for being the Savior-King who was bringing God's kingdom, and she was especially grateful that Jesus raised her brother from the dead (John 11). Take a minute to think about what you'd do if you experienced a miracle of that magnitude regarding a loved one.

Question 10. Jesus died to free you from sin and death. You have eternal life with God. That's worth wild gratitude, but we often take it for granted. We don't experience our freedom as vividly as Mary experienced her brother's resurrection. Don't cruise by this question lightly. Stop and give the group a chance to think about what Jesus has done for them.

Question 12. Wild gratitude day after day needs, among other things, daily reminders to ourselves of what Jesus has done. Daily thought given to that day's sins and need for forgiveness. Daily thoughts of the cross. Daily thought of the many things God provides: life, food, shelter, work, family, friends.

Question 13. You already have a couple of people handling worship during your meetings. They, or two other people, can take on the planning of this extended worship experience. You'll be amazed at how an experience like this can energize your group.

Question 6. Direct the group to the Study Notes so they'll understand what the cup is. Jesus' personal will or desire was to avoid the agony of torture, death, and especially the burden of the world's sin that would bring down the Father's avalanche of judgment upon him. This prayer for survival and the avoidance of pain reveals how completely human Jesus was. Self-sacrifice wasn't easy for him. It was just as painful as it would be for us. Yet Jesus accepted the pain because he loved the Father. Doing the Father's will was more important than self-preservation.

Question 7. We need to know that Jesus was fully human and faced the same temptation to resist the Father's painful will that we face (Hebrews 4:15). We mustn't overspiritualize Jesus and imagine that because he was the Son of God, surrender wasn't as wrenching for him as for us. Overspiritualizing leads us to take the crucifixion for granted, and it weakens our gratitude. God doesn't ask us to go through anything that Jesus didn't go through as a human.

Questions 9, 10, and 11. These questions are bound to elicit some anguished stories from group members who are facing tough situations in which they need to surrender to the Father's will. Other group members will be facing opportunities to serve God that are risky but positive. Avoid telling people what choices they should make. Listen to them, love them, and pray with them.

Questions 12 and 13. Be sure to save some time to look at these questions. It would be easy to let questions 9–11 take your whole meeting to an inward focus, but an outward focus is also essential.

Having one or more group members help launch a new group can be a turning point in the health of your group. You are the number-one factor in making it happen. We urge you to give serious consideration to question 13. We've worked with churches where group members took time out to launch new groups, and the results have been terrific. The old groups didn't fall apart; in fact, they were revitalized when members came back fired up by their experience of leadership. The boost in personal growth is huge. If you have just one couple willing to take this risk, give them every encouragement. Plan to pray for them and release them in session 6.

Ideally, you can pass leadership of your current group to someone else while you take a break to launch a new group. This will show the group you mean business about playing your part in fulfilling the Great Commission. The adventure begins here!

SESSION SIX:
VICTORY OVER DEATH

Whether your group is ending or continuing, it's important to celebrate where you have come together. If you choose not to discuss question 1 during your meeting, this would be a great question to discuss at a party. Be sure the spiritual partner time is honored.

Thank everyone for what they've contributed to the group. You might even give some thought ahead of time to something unique each person has contributed. You can say those things at the beginning of your meeting.

Question 3. Help your group to put themselves into the scene so that they experience Jesus' resurrection in a fresh way. This shouldn't be a dry doctrine; it will motivate you to surrender only to the degree that it's a vivid reality in your minds.

Question 6. This passage is often called "The Great Commission." Some of us prefer to think it applies to professional Christians, not us. But helping others become Jesus' disciples is one of the greatest catalysts for our own growth. Remind the group of what you learned in session 2 about the kernel of wheat that dies and bears fruit. You're not all called to be evangelistic preachers or small group leaders, but all of you can reproduce the life of Christ in another person's life over time. You can do this by helping to launch a new group or even by having lunch with one person and sharing what you've learned from this study. You can support missionaries and look for opportunities to talk about faith with the people you naturally encounter in your daily life. If you feel inadequate sharing your faith, why not make *Sharing Christ Together* your next study (assuming you haven't studied it already)? If Jesus really does have all authority in heaven and on earth, and if he really is with you always, then you don't need to be afraid.

Question 10. Some churches permit groups to celebrate Communion within their group. If yours does, this commemoration of Christ's death would be a meaningful event to wrap up your study or to include at your retreat. Otherwise, your group can attend a worship service together sometime when the Lord's Supper will be shared, and you can make this a group experience.

ABOUT THE AUTHORS

The authors' previous work as a team includes the DOING LIFE TOGETHER Bible study series, which won a Silver Medallion from the Evangelical Christian Publishers Association, as well as the DOING LIFE TOGETHER DVD series.

Brett Eastman has served as the champion of Small Groups and Leadership Development for both Willow Creek Community Church and Saddleback Valley Community Church. Brett is now the Founder and CEO of Lifetogether, a ministry whose mission is to "transform lives through community." Brett earned his Masters of Divinity degree from Talbot School of Theology and his Management Certificate from Kellogg School of Business at Northwestern University. **Dee Eastman** is the real hero in the family, who, after giving birth to Joshua and Breanna, gave birth to identical triplets—Meagan, Melody, and Michelle. They live in Las Flores, California.

Todd and Denise Wendorff serve at King's Harbor Church in Redondo Beach, California. Todd is a teaching pastor, handles leadership development, and pastors men. He is also coauthor of the Every Man Bible Study Series. Denise speaks to women at conferences, classes, and special events. She also serves women through personal discipleship. Previously, Todd was on the pastoral staff at Harvest Bible Chapel, Willow Creek Community Church, and Saddleback Valley Community Church. He holds a Th.M. from Talbot School of Theology. Todd and Denise live in Rolling Hills Estates, California with their three children, Brooke, Brittany, and Brandon.

Karen Lee-Thorp has written or cowritten more than fifty books and Bible studies, including *How to Ask Great Questions* and *Why Beauty Matters*. Her previous Silver Medallion winners are *The Story of Stories*, *LifeChange: Ephesians*, and *LifeChange: Revelation*. She was a senior editor at NavPress for many years and series editor for the LifeChange Bible study series. She is now a freelance writer, speaks at women's retreats, and trains small group leaders. She lives in Brea, California, with her husband, Greg Herr, and their daughters, Megan and Marissa.

SMALL GROUP ROSTER

Name	Address	Phone	Email Address	Team or Role	Church Ministry
Bill Jones	7 Almalar Street L.F. 92665	766-2255	bjones@aol.com	socials	children's ministry

(Pass your book around your group at your first meeting to get everyone's name and contact information.)

Name	Address	Phone	Email Address	Team or Role	Church Ministry

Experiencing Christ Together:
Living with Purpose in Community
Brett & Dee Eastman; Todd & Denise Wendorff;
Karen Lee-Thorp

Experiencing Christ Together: Living with Purpose in Community is a series of six, six-week study guides that offers small groups a chance to explore Jesus' teaching on the five biblical purposes of the church. By closely examining Christ's life and teaching in the Gospels, the series helps group members walk in the steps of Christ's early followers. Jesus lived every moment following God's purposes for his life, and Experiencing Christ Together helps groups learn how they can do this too. The first book lays the foundation: who Christ is and what he has done for us. Each of the other five books in the series looks at how Jesus trained his followers to live one of the five biblical purposes (fellowship, discipleship, service, evangelism, and worship).

	Softcovers	DVD
Beginning in Christ Together	ISBN: 0-310-24986-4	ISBN: 0-310-26187-2
Connecting in Christ Together	ISBN: 0-310-24981-3	ISBN: 0-310-26189-9
Growing in Christ Together	ISBN: 0-310-24985-6	ISBN: 0-310-26192-9
Serving Like Christ Together	ISBN: 0-310-24984-8	ISBN: 0-310-26194-5
Sharing Christ Together	ISBN: 0-310-24983-X	ISBN: 0-310-26196-1
Surrendering to Christ Together	ISBN: 0-310-24982-1	ISBN: 0-310-26198-8

Pick up a copy today at your favorite bookstore!

ZONDERVAN™

GRAND RAPIDS, MICHIGAN 49530 USA

WWW.ZONDERVAN.COM

life**together**.com